THE BUSINESS OF MUSIC

THE SONGWRITER'S AND MUSICIAN'S GUIDE TO MAKING GREAT DEMOS

Harvey Rachlin

Omnibus Press
London/New York/Sydney

To Syde Berman, who, with his Songwriter's Review, provided invaluable information and encouragement to budding tunesmiths for decades, and who published this writer's first articles and helped make his dream of becoming an author a reality.

First published by Writers Digest Books, Cincinnati, Ohio, USA.

©1988 Harvey Rachlin.
This edition © Copyright 1989 Omnibus Press
(A Division of Book Sales Limited)

Edited by Chris Barstow

Cover Designed by Pearce Marchbank

ISBN 0.7119. 1715.9

Order No: OP 45129

Exclusive distributors:
Book Sales Limited,
8/9 Frith Street,
London W1V 5TZ, UK.

Music Sales Corporation,
225 Park Avenue South,
New York, NY 10003, USA.

Music Sales Pty Limited,
120 Rothschild Avenue,
Rosebery, NSW 2018, Australia.

To the Music Trade only:
Music Sales Limited,
8/9 Frith Street,
London W1V 5TZ, UK.

Typeset by Rosemary Reay and Saxon Printing Ltd
Printed in England by
St. Edmundsbury Press Limited,
Bury St. Edmunds, Suffolk.

CONTENTS

TEN A FINAL WORD (OR TWO...)

ACKNOWLEDGMENTS

I am indebted to John Barilla and James Becher, who served as technical editors for this book. John, a sage of a recording engineer, and Jim, a synth and MIDI wizard, helped shape this book into its final form. Very special acknowledgement is due to David Copper. A most generous soul, David graciously and cheerfully spent hours proofreading the chapters and offered valuable suggestions and advice.

Special thanks is also due to Randy Battiste, who wholeheartedly shared his extensive knowledge of recording. With a 16-track recording studio in his bedroom, Randy is a dedicated songwriter/recordist and offered much valuable insight into home recording and other areas. Lachlan Westfall, President of the International MIDI Association, kindly imparted his wisdom on MIDI. Charlie Clouser was a valuable source of information on computers.

Gratitude is also extended to Victoria Lampkin, Khris Kellow, Jeff Burke, Henry Stephens, Sue Osborne, Robert Kandell, Craig Rachlin, and James D. Liddane. Various sections of the book improved under the attentive eyes of those who kindly performed proofreading chores: Steve DeFuria (another tech 'wonder'), Chas Clifton, Robert Fontana, Maxine Chrein, and Ben Rizzi.

No words could express my appreciation for my typist, Margaret Dyke. Her reliability and efficiency are beyond measure, her work is immaculate, and she is there at any hour to field my deluge of illegible manuscript pages. Margaret has been with me for years, and she helps make the arduous task of writing bearable!

I am grateful to Perry Knowlton of Curtis Brown Ltd.

With this book my new wife Marla quickly learned what a writer's life was like. But she benignly put up with the long hours of separation and offered all her support.

Finally, I would like to offer special thanks to the editor of this book, Julie Wesling Whaley. Indeed, the idea for the book originated with Julie, and I am grateful that she thought of me to write it. A most diligent editor, Julie called me regularly to discuss my progress, the music world and life in general. She is now not only my editor but my cherished friend as well.

Introduction

In this era of supersonic air travel, electronic banking and instant worldwide communication, something as seemingly innocent and imaginative as creating music has, alas, become engulfed by the tidal wave of modern technology. There is no need to mourn over music as a lost art, however. Machines (as we shall see later in this book) can launch writers into new dimensions, inspiring heavenly melodies and enabling composers to create endless textures and rhythms—interesting colorations of music and intoxicating grooves.

Not long ago (on the scale of human existence), songwriters were creative people who simply wrote songs. There's something romantic about the tunesmiths of yesteryear—whether they were minstrels wandering through the countryside introducing new ditties, or Tin Pan Alley writers secluded in some cubbyhole of an office penning sentimental pop ballads, comedy songs and syncopated tunes that would become overnight dance sensations. Indeed, today we might envy them more than a bit for living in uncomplicated times when songs about old mill streams caught the public's fancy, or when it was the steadfast desire of every proper man to 'want a girl just like the girl who married Dear Old Dad.'

Songwriters back then were interested in reaching into people's emotional pockets and effusing love, spirit and joy. (They were not unknown, however, to satirize, poke fun, or border on ribaldry.) And they had only simple tools to help them with their work—just their piano or guitar and a piece of paper and a pencil to record their compositions for posterity.

Modern technology has given rise to a new breed of songwriter: the hybrid creator. The composer of the 1980s is more likely to be an amalgamation of recording engineer, computer technician, 'one-man band,' vocalist, 'live' performer, arranger, producer, conductor, and ... oh yes, writer of songs. Today's writer wears many hats, and if you haven't tried any on for size yet then you're in for an awakening, not to mention a mild jolt!

If you are a songwriter who has just practised his craft by traditional methods, well, just be open-minded. Don't resist entering a land where the musical possibilities are out of this world.

It's not that the new instruments and equipment actually increase your creativity, it's that they help *you* to maximize it. By affording you various conveniences and possibilities (such as the ability to play back immediately multitrack recordings with rhythm, string and horn parts that you wrote, played and recorded yourself), modern machines can take you down new highways. When the scenery is different, so is the cruise.

Not sold yet? Suppose you're the type of person who just likes to sit down at a piano and peck out melodies or play chords with the left hand and search with the right for melodic lines that 'fit' the chords or may be superimposed harmoniously? Why should you have to change your ways? Well, for one thing, it's not as big a change as it seems. You can still play around with chords and little melodies. You can capture your ideas electronically and play them back with the push of a button. You can move the musical segments you like into more permanent storage or you can play with them and change them some more. Or they may spark new creative ideas. In the end, you'll be creating a sophisticated demo ready to compete in a tough marketplace.

Many songwriters today are pitching demos of such high quality that they're only a stone's throw away from commercial records. Budding artists submit tapes that are ready for release to record labels. It's a hit-or-miss proposition because if their product doesn't click then thousands of pounds may be wasted. But it's the only way they have a chance, because everybody else is doing the same thing.

It's happening all over the country, and 'major' and, 'independent' record companies alike are barraged with great demos.

You, too, have to be competitive. This could mean a complete overhaul of your writing methods, but as they say, 'Get with the times!' Today, devising sounds, grooves, rhythms and 'feels,' and recording them single-handedly is as much a part of the craft of songwriting as writing melodies and harmonies. Rest assured that once you master the equipment and techniques, you'll become hooked. You might even think your old ways of composing are archaic!

If you're inexperienced with electronics, or intimidated by them, don't worry. The techniques and principles can, for your purposes, be learned in a relatively short amount of time. You can certainly learn how to use the equipment without learning the intricacies of how it works. You need only take the time and interest to talk to informed sales people, ask enlightened friends questions, read books and articles, and experiment with the equipment until you understand how it works. (I hate to use clichés, but in this case 'practice makes perfect' is so applicable.) Once you have mastered the electronic end of songwriting (where would George Gershwin be today?), it will be a much more enjoyable, creative, and exciting process for you. The electronics will serve as a tool you can use to experiment with and to test musical ideas.

Today you don't have to play drums to be a drummer. You don't have to be an engineer to operate multitrack recording equipment. You needn't have studied music in a conservatory or previously cut records to arrange and produce. Strange as it sounds, you can do all these things with modern electronic instruments and equipment—if you want to.

Because songwriting is now somewhat of a technological endeavour, this book is by necessity technical. It goes in some detail into the theory and science of recording and creating musical sounds with contemporary instruments and devices. While your talents and interests may be primarily creative (in the pure sense), take the time to learn the material. It can only help you. Knowing how to showcase your songs better can only increase your chances of success.

Every attempt has been made to make this book as lucid as possible, and technical jargon has been kept to the minimum, but some jargon is still used, since becoming sophisticated and skilful in any area inevitably means using its terminology.

If you do not already own the instruments and equipment described here—synthesizers, drum machines, sequencers, computers, multitrack cassette recorders, signal processing equipment and MIDI gear—start saving your pennies. You don't have to run out tomorrow to start making your purchases, but if you're interested in making great demos, it's inevitable that you will eventually want to get some of the equipment discussed. There's no way around it—successful songwriting requires a commitment not only of time but also of money. Just remember this: it's an investment in *your* future!

CHAPTER ONE

THE BASICS

It starts with the song.

For all the glitter and glamour of the world of popular music—from international concert tours to outrageous clothing and cosmetics, from nationally televised award shows to slick videos with casts of provocative dancers—it begins with the interweaving of lyrics and music into a euphonious three-minute work of art. Indeed, after all is said and done in the record biz, it comes *down* to the song. In an arena characterized by a 'survival of the fittest' code of competition, only recordings embodying the best, most commercial songs succeed.

A song, in and of itself, is an intangible property. It can be reproduced and communicated in various forms—audio, video and print among them—but has no substance of itself *per se*. It's a long and winding road to bring an idea, a concept, a musical creation from your home to those of people around the world, but there is a universal way to begin.

You start with a demo.

With a demo you can expose your song to an unlimited number of people who might be in a position to record it or get it recorded—from artists and producers to publishers and record company executives. It is your sales tool—your résumée and business plan wrapped up into one neat package. It is a make-or-break commodity, for ultimately you will be judged on one criterion alone: content. This means the song, but the song will be framed by an arrangement and production, and these elements must showcase the work to its best advantage.

Obviously, great care must be given to the making of your demo. This encompasses two basic stages—planning, and carrying out your creative ideas in the recording/mixing processes. These should be attended to with the utmost diligence, because today, with high-tech musical and electronic equipment available for consumers at affordable prices, demos have reached a considerable level of sophistication.

What is a demo? A demo is a relatively inexpensive and not-completely-produced recording made to show the potential of a musical composition or the talent of a person. It can be used to showcase such works and abilities as:

songs
jingles
show scores
voices
performances
arranging skills
production skills
engineering abilities

A demo can be almost anything, depending upon the particular use for which it is intended or designed. It can be used to demonstrate a creation, a talent, a skill...anything.

The ultimate goal in making a demo is to 'sell' something: to get a song commercially recorded, to get hired for a particular job, to obtain 'angels' to back a certain production, or whatever else, as the case may be. Traditionally, the most common use of demos has been to interest artists and producers in recording songs or to showcase bands to record companies.

Demos range widely in terms of production. At one end of the scale there is the simplest type, a vocal/instrument (piano or guitar) demo recorded in mono. At the other extreme is the stereo multitrack rendition with signal processing. (This may be something close to a master quality tape or a recording that can be made into a master with the addition of new tracks and further mixing.) There are various factors to be considered in determining the elaborateness of the demo you need, and these will be discussed later. Essentially, you'll want to make a demo that will best showcase your song within your means.

The term *demo* may actually refer to either (1) a sound recording or (2) the physical medium embodying a sound recording, such as a cassette tape, reel-to-reel tape or disk. Videotapes are not in general used to present songs, although some unsigned artists use them to showcase both their bands and their original material. (This is not always necessary, however, for most companies will accept an audiotape and a photo.) Storage mediums are constantly improving, and DAT (Digital Audio Tape) has already brought digital cassette mastering within reach of the semi-pro market; in the future, other modernistic software may be used to present demos.

Since most readers of this book will be primarily interested in getting their songs commercially recorded, the discussions that follow will focus on that area, but the material is, of course, applicable to any musical property or skill.

The market reality

Okay, you've just completed this musical masterpiece, it's the best thing you've ever done, and you're eager to launch it to its rightful place—the top of the charts. It's so much better than what you hear on the radio. If only Bruce Springsteen or Whitney Houston would record it, you know—you just know!—it would become a hit.

This is a common sentiment among amateur and professional songwriters alike. It may often be true that major artists could make hits out of the unpublished material waiting to find a voice. But there are several reasons why a song with genuine potential might not enjoy the successful commercial recording it deserves: it doesn't get heard by the 'right' person; its arrangement or production on the demo is lacking; the publishing rights aren't available to the parties concerned; it doesn't 'fit' the style of those recording artists to whom it was presented. Many artists are self-contained (write and sometimes produce their own songs) and generally will not record 'outside' material written by someone else.

The problem for songwriters is the market reality: only a small percentage of the songs written each year can be commercially released. There are only so many artists with contracts, and only so many who record outside material; there can be only so many tunes put on an album and only so many cuts distributed and promoted as singles; there are only so many records the public will buy. The last factor is the most suppressing. The size (and demographics) of the record-buying public limits the amount of music that can be marketed successfully. It's the old 'supply and demand' principle.

How do some songs succeed?

Music consumption, like that of other commercial industries, is large but limited. Only the best 'products' succeed, although in music, public taste is more subjective than objective about what is 'the best.' But then again, the public can only buy what's on the market, and that's determined, for the most part, by the industry forces—A& R people and executives of record companies who decide what records to release, and radio station music and programme directors who select what records to play. These forces draw from a pool of creators that includes you. It is a group in which your colleagues and competitors are the likes of Bruce Springsteen, Paul McCartney, Billy Joel, Carly Simon, Dolly Parton, Stevie Wonder, Prince, and David Bowie. With competition as keen as that, you cannot afford not to put your best foot forward. And assuming you have talent (which invariably requires much practice of the songwriting craft), you can succeed. Classic songwriter/artists like those just mentioned have no secret or magic, but they have a deep love for music, appreciate the endless possibilities for pop songs, and have worked very hard at their craft. They weren't born stars but at one point in their lives discovered an interest and maximized their talent.

Few writers can consistently make the charts through the years. New writers can, and consistently do, break in. The industry needs new creative blood, and unproven writers willing to go about their business intelligently and methodically (not to mention persistently) *can* be heard, widely and loudly!

Finally, faith and confidence also play a role in a song's placement. You've got to approach writing with the belief that a quality song will find a home. Indeed, that aphorism is probably true more often than not.

When to make a demo

This will depend on the instruments and equipment you have. If you have a synthesizer, drum machine, and 4-track cassette tape recorder, you can actually be making a demo tape at the same time that you're writing a song! As you experiment with new lines, you can keep or dispose of them as you wish. You're actually working out a song on tape as you go along, and when you're finished, you have a complete demo. (More about this in Chapter Seven, 'Home Recording'.) You can record all your ideas and piece together a demo at any time, when a song is rough or finished, without any cost except for tape (excluding your investment in the hardware).

If you have a home studio, then theoretically you could demo each and every tune you pen. But you should seriously consider the time factor. To demo every song or idea is wasteful because not every composition is going to have strong commercial potential. You should not confuse making a demo with the practice (and a good one at that) of some writers who leave a tape recorder (usually just a portable cassette) running while they are creating, improvising, experimenting with, or working out ideas at their instrument. Time is a most valuable commodity. It should be used prudently. Time may be better spent in creating new, commercial songs than in demoing a song that has little chance of being placed with an artist or producer.

If you don't have instruments and equipment at home, you can make your demos in a recording studio, or in the home of someone who does have the proper equipment. But in those cases, you will have to be judicious when it comes to booking studio time, musicians and vocalists. Because costs have the potential to mount rapidly, song selection is the key factor. If you do not have a song that you think is worthy of recording (and of your money), wait until you do. And consider this: the money you put out would probably be better spent on the instruments and equipment that would allow you to record demos right in your own home. Don't worry about learning the technology. Salespeople will be happy to spend the time you need to acquire a working knowledge of the equipment.

Whether you record in a professional studio or at home, there is one fundamental rule in regard to those tunes you will spend a lot of time on and intend to shop to industry people: make orchestrated, quality demos only of those songs that you feel have commercial potential.

A word about the term *commercial*, which you'll read here frequently and often hear in discussions about the industry. To many it has a negative connotation—and for a songwriter like yourself who wants to write hits, it shouldn't. You want to 'sell' your songs to a music publisher, record producer, artist, or record company. That means somebody or some entity is going to have to put money behind your song in the belief that, in professionally recorded form, people are going to buy it in quantity—hopefully enough to make a handsome profit. When a product has the potential to be, or has in fact been marketed successfully, it is considered commercial. It appeals to the masses, period! There's nothing dirty about the word.

If you're in this for a career, don't waste time with songs that are sure tickets to nowhere. As a writer (and not a recording artist), you have to supply hits or 'singles.' Producers are not looking for filler or album cuts: those *they* write! You're there to give them what they can't come up with themselves!

Choosing the songs

Because eager songwriters are generally prolific, churning out song after song after song, it often becomes difficult for them to decide which are worthy of making into demos. Some songs will capture the writer's personal preference, but they may not always be the most commercially viable. We've all heard stories about those tunes on the bottom of the list that turned out to be the buried dynamite that rocketed a writer to fame and riches.

When you want to demo your next song, consider the following questions: Would an established artist be likely to record the song? Who would it be suitable for? Is the song 'happening' for today's market? How do you think it would sell to the public if it were released? Factors such as personal taste, instinct and knowledge of the market will help you answer these and similar questions. But the questions need to be answered as honestly and objectively as possible.

As the creator of a work of art, your vision might be clouded. You will be inspecting your song through the same pair of eyes that a parent views his or her child. It may appear marvellous to you, but not so to a random passer-by. Because your new song is the product of your imagination and talent, you will inevitably love it. Otherwise, you really wouldn't have spent so much time writing, rewriting, perfecting and completing the song, would you? But will other, more objective people love it as much? This is said not to be discouraging but to prompt you to be selective, since the effort to make a good demo is considerable (and perhaps costly), and time might be better spent back at the drawing board. Unfortunately, many songwriters make demos of songs that stand no chance of getting placed, and waste a lot of their hard-earned cash.

To select the best of your songs, it is usually beneficial to obtain feedback from others whose opinions you respect and trust. To gauge the opinions of others, you can perform a song live or make a preliminary demo, or 'pre-demo.' A pre-demo is a simple recording made just to show how a song goes. If you don't have semi-pro equipment at home, you can make a pre-demo on a portable cassette tape recorder. If you don't have one (heaven forbid!), borrow one from a friend. You or somebody else can play on piano or guitar and sing the song. In very, very few cases such demos may be adequate for submission purposes, but today with competition the way it is—fancy 8- and 16-track demos—your chances for success are much greater with a recording comparable in production and quality.

A trap some writers fall into, though, is to think that if a forty-piece orchestra and a group of backing vocalists were behind a recording of their song, it would necessarily be a hit. Quantity is not quality. The song in raw form—that is, stripped of strings, brass, and percussion lines to a bare melody (and lyric)—must be good, very good. Often, however (and this usually comes when the musical output is high), it is difficult to determine which of your songs are the best or which have the most potential.

There may be times when you play a song that you're particularly fond of and receive only a lukewarm response. You may be discouraged, or your belief in the song might remain undiminished, leading you to think that only a finished demo would bring out what you 'hear.' Ultimately you will be the judge, and you will probably go along with your own instincts.

Remember, not every song you're going to write will be tomorrow's chart topper. You're working at your craft all the time, and no matter how successful you become, you'll still be honing your craft. No artist reaches a degree of excellence where everything turned out is perfect. We're only human, after all.

Planning

Making a demo is like dressing up for a job interview. You take care over appearance because you want to make the most favourable impression possible. If your demo gets hired (signed by a music publishing company), there might be a probationary period in which you must continue to sell it (to artists and record producers). Once this is accomplished, you will be given the opportunity to 'prove' your appeal to the public, that is, your song will be sent out in full and radiant attire: a master recording.

After you've made the decision to demo a particular song, you must plan how you want to dress it up to make the impression you want. This stage comprises creative planning and what we'll call pre-production administration, which applies mostly to writers who will not be recording on home equipment.

First, a concept must be planned, an idea of what kind of arrangement and production you want to showcase the song. While the concepts of some songs seem naturally to dictate themselves, the elaborateness of arrangement and production will depend upon certain factors: the style of the song or what genre you want it to fit, the particular sound you want it to have, the current sound of the day's chart-makers, whether you have a particular artist in mind to record it, and how much money you have to spend (if you are renting a studio and hiring musicians).

Genre

Classify your song. Is it pop, rock, country, rhythm and blues, dance music, Latin, folk, jazz? Each of these musical styles dictates certain instrumentations, orchestrations and 'feels' and you will incorporate these into your recording. This is not to say that you will be simulating previous arrangements—you can be quite creative here—but the genre you choose will give you a general direction.

The 'sound' of your song is another major consideration. Your demo should have the 'groove' of what's happening today, not ten years ago or even five years ago. Although the master recording of your song will ultimately give it its feel, the person auditioning your tune might not have the 'ears' (imagination) to hear or envision it in a revamped, contemporary arrangement. Top 40 radio stations, or whatever designation contemporary hit music broadcasters use, want to programme records with sounds that are progressive and trend-setting, not dated. While it is an industry axiom that a terrific song, no matter how dated, will find an audience, the same is not necessarily true for a recording with a dated production.

With the synthesizer, computer and numerous other products continually being updated (and new products being introduced often outdating very recent equipment), a variety of sounds can be achieved and recorded efficiently. As a songwriter you should be familiar with these sounds, if you are not already.

The vocalist

Who should sing on your demo? If you can carry a tune well or if you're also trying to sell yourself as an artist, then naturally you will sing. But while many writers possess a melodic gift, they were short-changed in the vocal department. They need singers for their demos.

You should always use the best singer you can find, or one who performs very well in the style of your song. If you have trouble finding good singers in your area, you might try calling the music department of a high school or college for a recommendation, advertising in a local paper or at a nearby music store, or asking at a recording studio.

There is also the consideration of whether the lyrics demand a male or female singer. You wouldn't want a vocalist singing a love ballad to someone of the same sex. When deciding whether a man should sing about 'her' or a woman sing about 'him,' consider what naturally sounds better and/or to whom you will be pitching the song. It's usually best to have a song as generically neutral as possible.

Casting your song

It's quite probable that you might have a certain recording artist in mind before you demo your song. In an effort to show how well suited the tune is for that artist, some unpublished writers try to get a singer to simulate that particular artist's style on the demo.

This is usually not a wise move. The artist may not find it a flattering imitation! Also, you don't want to pin all your hopes on one singer. If you send your song out to many markets, the one that finally accepts it may be one you thought was a long-shot. It's best to make your demo as neutral as possible, to show that it will be a good song no matter who records it. There is more information about casting in Chapter Eight, 'Submitting Your Demos.'

The songs on your demo tape

At the end of your recording session, you will end up with one or more songs on tape. Your mixed down, 2-track, stereo tape recording, or your original tape recording, is your master. You will make copies from it. The tape copy containing one or more songs is called a demo or a demo tape.

How many songs do you include on each demo tape? If you've only recorded one song, should you send that out alone or wait until you've recorded others? There's nothing wrong with sending out one song, if it's terrific. Some songwriters prefer to shop songs one at a time, thinking that a demo with one title professionally declares, 'This is the one song for you!' If your song doesn't have the potential to be a hit single, though, it's better to wait until you write and record songs that do. Generally, you should include no more than three or four songs on a demo, and they should all be very commercial. Put your best song first.

If you're going to include three or four songs on your demo tape, it's best to have the majority as uptempo numbers and only one ballad, unless you feel you have two slow songs that are smashes. Artists and producers are generally more interested in finding lively tunes with hit potential.

If you write in a variety of musical styles and are submitting directly to an artist or producer, don't mix songs of different genres on the same tape. In other words, don't submit a tape of a country song, a rock tune and an R& B song. If you're trying to interest a listener in recording your tune, he'll only be interested in songs of the genre he's been successful in. But this is not a definitive rule. A country singer, for instance, might hear a pop tune he likes and want to cut it in a country arrangement. Also if you're trying to show your songwriting talent and versatility to a music publisher, who approaches artists of different musical genres, then you could submit a tape with different kinds of songs on it. But they'd better be good! Trying to show off your versatility just for the sake of it could repel a listener.

Intros

Most pop songs have introductions. Limit yours to four bars. Amateur songwriters sometimes use long intros to their tunes, and this can be a turnoff to industry professionals who listen to a lot of material. Knee-deep in piles of song tapes and short on time, these people want to hear the essence of the song as soon as possible. When they hear something that doesn't excite them, they stop playing the song. Forget about them listening to the entire tune!

Solos

Generally, long solos should be avoided in demos. Listeners are interested in hearing the potential of a song, not the virtuosity of a musician. Sometimes, however, it might be all right for an instrument to play the melody (after it has been sung) for variety. Also, for certain types of music like hard rock, long instrumental breaks are common. But if you've written a regular pop song, either leave out an instrumental solo in your demo or keep it short.

Endings

How do you end your song? That might depend on the kind of song it is. If it has a hook to it, end with the hook repeating and gradually fading out. This will help the hook last as long as possible in the listener's mind. If it is a ballad, you'll want to end with a big climax, where the sounds—the last word (or syllable) and the music—sustain for a few seconds. Occasionally, songs end abruptly, but if you consider an abrupt ending, ask yourself why or how it would enhance the song. There are no definitive or universal rules on how to end a song, but certain styles lend themselves to certain arrangements. Listen to the radio and learn.

Arrangers and musicians

Now let's address the arrangement, performance and production of the demo. If you own a synthesizer, drum machine, sequencer, and multitrack tape recorder, you can create great arrangements and productions even if your musical training and experience are limited. If you do not own these instruments and equipment and are not able to conceptualize a musical arrangement, do not despair. There are many capable persons available for hire.

If you need to hire an arranger, or musicians and vocalists, you can find them, among other places, through music paper ads, music shops, clubs, record shops, the classified telephone directory, and any venues where musicians are engaged. Be sure to find those who are suited to the type of music you write. You might interest a group you like that plays at a local club in doing your tunes. They are probably into writing their own material too, but there needn't be any feelings of competition. They will only be recording your material for demonstration purposes. You can negotiate fees. If the group likes one of your songs well enough to include it on their demo or in their club date act, then that's a nice bonus for you!

How do you convey your song to an arranger (such as a student, capable musician-friend, professional) or musicians and vocalists? You can sing it (unless your voice is so horrid it would confuse them) as well as discuss it. As mentioned previously, you can make a 'preliminary demo,' and the participants can use this to learn the song. Or you can make a lead sheet (see page 19). A talented musician who can also arrange will be invaluable to your recording session. You would only need to convey your ideas to this one person and he or she could handle all other details, injecting personal creativity. This person might devise an arrangement that you would never even have thought of that would please you very much. If you don't know of a capable musician, ask around or inquire at music shops, or look in the Yellow Pages under 'Music arrangers and composers.'

Preparation Hiring musicians to record your song can be a harrowing experience if you're trying desperately to show them how you want it to be played and they're just making a mess of it. You had a 'vision' for your song that you hoped the musicians would capture, and all you come away with is frustration and disappointment. It's especially upsetting if you've paid for studio time, and the clock is ticking furiously away!

To prevent this, you must convey your interpretation of the song to the musicians and vocalists. Be as sure as you can be that they understand what you want *before* they begin to record. You'll have a lot more peace of mind, and you'll minimize the time it takes (and money in the studio) to get the demo you want.

Of course, you'll want to hire competent musicians and singers. Studio performers who make masters are usually so well trained that they can sight-read an original piece of material at a session and, after going over it once or twice, play it perfectly for recording. While the musicians you use on your demo *may* be of such calibre, you're usually better off giving them a lead sheet or tape of the song in advance, so they can learn it perfectly for the session and perhaps throw in a few ideas of their own. Allow the musicians and singers room to breathe some life into your songs through their own interpretations. More often than not they'll enhance your tune. And be sure to make it easy for your singers by typing or printing neatly on a separate sheet the words to your song.

The lead sheet

Lead sheets are the functional predecessors of demos. Prior to and for several decades after the advent of recording in the late 1870s, songwriters wrote out their tunes on manuscript paper. If a song was accepted by a music publisher, the publisher would print sheet music of it and dispatch a 'song-plugger' to musical instrument shops and other retailers. The song-plugger would play the tune on the piano, and hopefully that would motivate customers to purchase the sheet music. Today, music publishers and record company people often cannot even read music, and if they could, they might interpret a song differently from what the songwriter had in mind. So demos are a better (albeit a more expensive) way to present a song. You at least control how the song is interpreted and how the listener hears it. But lead sheets have not fallen into oblivion as yet, and do serve a few different purposes, so you might want to write them (or have others write them) for your songs.

A lead sheet is a manuscript notation of your song. It contains the melody, with the lyrics printed below and the chords above. On the music paper should also be the title of the song (at the top, of course), the name(s) of the composer(s) and lyricist(s), musical directions such as the tempo, and the copyright notice, which generally appears at the bottom of the first page. It is not necessary to submit a piano arrangement of your song. The melody line with lyrics and chords will suffice, should you choose to submit a lead sheet.

A lead sheet may also be used as proof of authorship. More information on this is given in Chapter 8, 'Submitting Your Demos'.

Many arrangers use a lead sheet when writing out the instrumental parts of a song. While some songs today are recorded with electronic instruments, and the parts worked out by ear, others may be recorded by large ensembles of musicians who read off chord charts. In writing out the chart, the arranger works from a lead sheet of the song.

As stated earlier in this chapter, lead sheets may also be used to teach your song to others. For writers who can't carry a tune to save their lives, a lead sheet is a good starting point in trying to convey your musical creation. Once others get the general idea of how your song goes, you can refine their interpretation by explaining how you want certain sections to go, or even by venturing to bellow out some parts.

Finally, lead sheets are handy for reference or pleasure on the songwriter's piano or music shelf. If you can read music and you want to play a song, having a lead sheet enables you to play it right away. You can play it for pleasure, to show others, or to rework the song. You may write a tune or part of a tune and come back to it years later and be inspired to improve or finish it. Songwriters of decades past were known to leave unfinished or undiscovered gems in their trunks. So as you can see, lead sheets can be of importance to you, but you're still better off putting more time into perfecting your demo. In today's market, it is the demo that sells the song.

Getting it going At this point, let us assume that you have selected the song you wish to record and have a fairly good idea of the creative direction in which you want to go with respect to recording it. You've done some planning and preparation work. It's time for action.

Where do you record it?

Where do you plan to record your demo? If you have multitrack tape recording equipment at home, then of course you will want to do it there. If you do not own quality recording equipment (or have a friend who does), you will be booking time in a recording studio. You could record in a commercial recording studio or in a smaller, demo-orientated facility. The former may have a smaller room for making demos. The latter usually offers excellent equipment and is available, of course, at cheaper prices because operation and overhead costs are lower. Detailed information on what to consider when shopping for a studio appears in Chapter Two, 'Multitrack Recording and Mixing.'

It's easy to find a studio; almost every local area has at least one. Look in your Yellow Pages or check the music papers for ads or articles. If you still cannot find one, try asking at your local music shop. Should your locale actually not have a studio, you will have to look further afield.

Costs

The next consideration is costs. Studio rates for making 8- or 16-track recordings (sufficient for demos) range from as little as 10 pounds to 50 pounds or more per hour. Then you have to pay for musicians and vocalists (assuming that you need them); this could range from free (a favour) to 60 pounds or more per session. There might be additional expenses incurred for rental of certain musical instruments and outboard gear for signal processing. Finally, there are mixing and tape costs. All together, the cost of demoing a single song at a commercial studio could quite easily run into several hundred pounds.

Call up studios and request rate cards. These will give you an idea of the range of studio rates. Be aware, however, that studio rates are often negotiable. If you record in 'down time,' when the studio has unbooked hours between sessions, or in off-hours during the evening, you might be able to agree a lower rate. Studios usually lower the rate, too, when blocks of time are reserved; but because you will be making only a demo, the time you need will (or should) be limited.

You shouldn't have to worry about hiring an engineer—this technician normally comes with the studio rental. Engineers vary in ability but most are perfectly competent. Some recording artists are quite finicky about who engineers their sessions, and they bring in those they have worked with before, trust, and have confidence in. But they are making master recordings. You don't have to worry about state-of-the-art engineering. As long as the equipment is in good working order and the engineer has had experience working the controls, then you're in good shape. But he or she should be capable enough to apprise you of your options with regard to special techniques and signal processing.

Unless your best friend has a home studio and will let you use it any time for free, there's no way around spending money to further your career as a songwriter—that is, to demo your tunes. You're going to have to spend money, whether it's to rent a studio and pay musicians, or to buy the equipment you need to make the demos at home yourself (the latter, once again, a more judicious option).

True, songwriters generally don't have much money, but it should be understood that a career in songwriting requires an investment. So if it costs you up to a few thousand pounds while you're trying to make it as a songwriter, consider it an investment in your career. Making demos and submitting them are a major part of a songwriter's education. While it is more difficult to make it in songwriting than in many other professions, the rewards and personal satisfaction from it are, at least from this prejudiced writer's point of view, far, far greater. And you can enjoy a life of creating, bringing joy to others, and getting a thrill out of hearing people sing or whistle your songs, or knowing that people are buying records of them.

It should be said that if you can interest a music publisher in your work and talent, an arrangement may be set up where you, whether hired as a 'staff writer' or not, may be able to use recording facilities owned by the company or rented by the company for you.

Who pays for the demo?

If you do not have the money to buy recording equipment or make a demo at a commercial studio, wait until you do. Or perhaps you could even borrow from a close relative or friend. But do not—repeat, *do not*—sell 'shares' in your song or give away publishing rights or percentages for a loan of a few hundred pounds. If you think your song is good enough to demo, then it might have real potential. This could eventually translate into many, many thousands of pounds, and it would be a shame to lose part of the money, not to mention copyright ownership or control, due to a lean period.

Of course, if a publisher is financing your demo and allowing you to use the company's facilities (as discussed earlier), he will expect to receive a percentage of the publishing revenue. Publishers naturally prefer to own copyrights themselves, but you should aim to negotiate a 'licence' deal, under which the publisher has exclusive rights to exploit your material for a limited period of time—e.g. three years. (Whatever the deal, try to check that the company is a *bona fide* organization, make sure that you see the terms in writing, and preferably get a lawyer to check over them, although this could be expensive.) After the demo is completed, you will have the company's services in trying to get your song placed with a signed artist. The costs of making the demo, placing the song, and administering it (copyright registration and contractual paperwork) are the firm's investment in your work; that is why publishers get a share of publishing revenue (traditionally, 50 percent of the song's income, but increasingly, as little as 15 percent). While on the subject, it must be said that if you do sign away your copyright to a publisher, you should try to get a 'reversion right' to your song; that is, if it is not placed within a specified time period, the rights to the song go back (revert) to you. This will be more difficult to do if you're a staff writer or receive a cash advance from the publisher to record the demo, because publishers won't want to give up a song they've invested in.

The completed demo

Your completed demo should represent in your mind a terrific showcase for your song. It may be a very simple recording, leaving an artist or producer much room for styling in a creative and individual way. Or it may be a very orchestrated piece of work, with many lines and background accompaniment. This more complete demo ensures that whoever auditions the song will be able to 'hear' its potential, whereas he may have been unable to imagine a finished production from a somewhat rough demo of a new, original song. Whatever method you choose, just be sure you are happy with the results before submitting it. Sounds simple, but writers are often hasty in demoing their work, eager to get it on tape so that they can send it out as soon as possible. Taking the time to do the demo completely to your satisfaction might make all the difference in the world.

Demo sessions and the unions

There are trade unions in the entertainment industry that serve to protect members' rights, just as there are unions functioning in most other industries. With respect to recording, the Musicians' Union and the actors' association, Equity, have minimum contracts for musicians and singers who participate in master recordings. (The MU represents singers as well as musicians, but some singers—particularly those specializing in stage work—are represented by Equity.) The contracts are very detailed, and provide for a minimum scale and other terms relating to working conditions and employment.

Since rates of engagement are related to the end use, however, there are no minimum terms of employment laid down in relation to demos. But if the demo is going to be high-quality, and could potentially be used as a commercial master, your musicians and singers may well expect to be paid as for a standard recording session. Check the going rates with your local branches of MU and Equity.

In conclusion...

The process of making a demo involves the following:

1. Complete a song to your satisfaction.
2. Come up with an arrangement or get someone who will do this for you. (If you are recording on home equipment, you may want to work this out yourself.)
3. Hire musicians and a singer (or whatever performers you need) to make your demo.

4. Provide a pre-demo or lead sheet to anyone who will be recording your song and be sure he or she knows it well before going into the studio.
5. Book studio time.
6. Record your song.
7. Make copies from your master.

It must be emphasized that the above would apply to traditional demos made in the studio with 'live' musicians. Today, many songwriters have electronic instruments and recording equipment and make demos by themselves at home. They record finished songs, or work ideas and sounds out as they go along.

CHAPTER TWO

MULTITRACK RECORDING AND MIXING

Today, demos have reached such a high level of quality that there's often a thin line between demos and masters. Musically, their arrangements and production are dynamic and creative. Technically, their fidelity is crisp and clear, with the timbres of the various musical instruments and voices enhanced by electronic effects. While demos should leave something to the imagination so that artists, arrangers and producers may inject their own originality, it generally becomes necessary, in order to become competitive, to make a demo that is a high-calibre recording of a song.

What this means to you, the songwriter, is that you have to go multitrack. This will help your demos be competitive with others. Your demo may land in a pile with dozens of others and what often sticks out first is the quality of the production—the arrangement and the audio fidelity. Your demo will invariably be competing with others into which much time and effort has been put trying to create recordings that are as professional as possible, with all sorts of effects added to enhance the audio and performance qualities of the songs. By knowing the techniques of multitrack recording you'll be less reliant on others to arrange and produce your tunes and more capable of recording songs yourself. Indeed, understanding the techniques will enable you to be in a home or professional studio and know the way things will be done, how to get the best recording. and what alternatives you may have.

As a serious, committed songwriter, you have to learn about multitrack recording. It will enable you to do more with your song—to build on it, repair it, develop it further—everything you need to know to present it as you conceive it. It will afford you flexibility, variety, convenience and control, and enable you to shape your songs to their best advantage.

What is multitrack recording? Multitrack recording is a process in which instruments and voices are recorded individually or in ensemble onto separate storage bands (tracks) of a tape, which are aligned physically, to give the effect during playback that the musical parts were recorded simultaneously. Through another process called mixing, the levels of all the instruments and voices may be adjusted relative to one another to create a desired balance. Signal processing (modification of audio signals) is performed both during recording and mixing to enhance the quality of the sounds. The final product is always a 2-track (stereo) recording.

Multitrack recording is the method by which commercial records and top-quality demos are creatively produced. It requires separate stages (usually separate sessions) in which musicians and singers record their parts. Ultimately there is a whole recording that—with special effects added during both the track-by-track recording and the 'mixdown' (that is, mixing all the separate tracks together onto the final, 2-track master)—is greater than the sum of its parts.

Open-reel tapes used for multitrack recording come in a variety of sizes—$\frac{1}{4}$-inch, $\frac{1}{2}$-inch, 1-inch, and 2-inch. (There are also multitrack cassette tapes which are $\frac{1}{8}$-inch and $\frac{1}{2}$-inch). The larger open-reel tapes are used to record a greater number of tracks, although today as many as eight different tracks can be recorded on a magnetic tape only $\frac{1}{8}$-inch in width. The tapes themselves don't come with subdivided bands; rather, sound information is magnetically infused onto the tape by the recording heads of the tape recorder. The recorded information is stored as horizontally aligned bands that correspond to the alignment of the heads. Fig. 1 shows the recording heads of 4-, 8- and 16-track tape recorders.

The more tracks available, the more individual sounds that can be recorded. This allows you to add more parts ('overdubs') and enhance the sound of your recording. After all, a 50-piece orchestra sounds better and fuller than one with only 15 musicians. Multi-track recording also allows you to further improve the sound levels and colorations of the different instruments and voices after they have been recorded.

Fig. 1 RECORDING HEADS

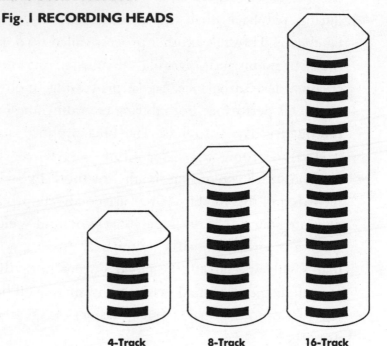

4-Track   8-Track   16-Track

Diagram by David Copper

How sound is recorded onto magnetic tape

Sound is recorded onto tape by an electromagnetic process as magnetic tape moves past the record head of the tape recorder. The term 'magnetic tape' doesn't mean that the tape inherently contains a magnetic field, but that it is capable of being magnetized by the magnetic field present at the record head. Magnetic tape consists of a clear film base on which there is a mixture of magnetic particles made up of gamma ferric oxide and various additives. This mixture forms a kind of 'magnetic paint' that is applied to the plastic base in what is called the coating process.

Each particle on the tape has a north and a south pole. During recording, a signal (that is, an electrical current—in the case of 'live' recording, converted from acoustical energy to electrical energy within the microphone) goes through the circuitry of the tape recorder and travels to the record head, where it magnetizes the tape. The record head is basically a coil surrounded by a special core that creates a magnetic field when an electrical current flows through it. When the tape moves into this magnetic field, the electronic signal becomes imbedded in the magnetic particles. The amount of magnetism applied, or energy induced by the record head, is proportional to the imprint of the information on the magnetic particles. As a simple analogy, think of putting your foot into wet cement. If you step on it lightly, you'll make a slight or moderate indentation. If you step on it hard and grind your foot into it, you'll make a substantial indentation. Getting back to our subject, when the tape is played back, the reproduce head 'reads' the magnetism on the tape and, through special electronic circuits, decodes the signal for amplification to the speakers (where it is converted back from electrical energy to acoustical sound—the opposite of what a microphone does).

Why a good quality tape is needed

You could have written the most sensational song, but if the audio fidelity is poor, then chances are it will be rejected on the spot. It's difficult enough to determine a hit when all things are right, but when the fidelity of a recording of an original song is such that the words and music are not entirely discernible, it can completely destroy the creative effort. Furthermore, a poorly recorded tape will psychologically turn off listeners. They will think that if the writer didn't take the time and effort to record a composition properly, then he couldn't have been very excited about it in the first place.

Make the effort to create the clearest sound possible. This may seem like common sense, but unfortunately, many amateur song-writers submit demos that sound as if they were recorded on portable cassettes with the dishwasher, clothes dryer and television running in the background! Just ask any music publisher or A& R person—they all have stories to tell! A better-made demo will receive more respect and attention, and with all the quality demos (soundwise) floating around, it becomes necessary for you to send out a recording that is bright and clean.

Studio recording vs. home recording

Multitrack recordings have traditionally been made in the studio. However, with the manufacturing of semi-pro quality equipment at affordable prices in recent years, the process is increasingly being done in the home. This means that by purchasing equipment such as a 4-track cassette tape recorder, you can make quality multitrack recordings in your bedroom! While the difference between studio and home recording is essentially one of sound quality (although some home recordists would play down the difference), the methods of recording are essentially the same: the basic tracks are laid and then followed by the overdubs. The final result, a multitrack tape recording, is mixed down to a 2-track stereo tape from which copies can be made.

Methods of multitrack recording

There are two basic methods of recording pop music: 'live' (the traditional process) and electronic. The latter process has developed with the application of computer technology to recording.

Electronic recording

Electronic recording utilizes devices such as sequencers, syn-thesizers and drum machines: it also enables an individual to lay down all the tracks of a recording without the use of other musicians. Songwriters and musicians who own the electronic recording equipment can make quality demos in their very own homes. Electronic recording is covered in Chapter Seven, 'Home Recording.'

How pop records are made with 'live' musicians

A typical professional pop record with 'live' musicians (as opposed to a record made with the parts programmed on MIDI sequencers, which are discussed in Chapter 5) will take several sessions to make. A 'live' session in pop music typically works in the following way.

First, a rhythm section lays down (records) the basic tracks. Basic tracks are the foundation over which other instrumentalists and vocalists record. The rhythm section generally consists of keyboard, drums, guitar and bass guitar. The number of tracks the rhythm section takes up depends on how many tracks will be used for the entire recording, the preferences of the producer (songwriter), and other factors. If sixteen or more tracks are going to be used, a rhythm section usually takes up from four to eight tracks.

In recording the basic tracks, a vocalist sings the song to guide the musicians. This rendition is called a 'guide vocal,' and is usually not used as the final lead vocal. The singer usually records his or her part after all the tracks have been recorded.

After the basic tracks are laid down, the process of overdubbing begins. In overdubbing, the basic tracks are played back while musicians and vocalists record new parts in synchronization with the existing ones as they listen to them. The previously recorded tracks may be heard through headphones or,if the musician is recording with an instrument (such as a synthesizer) that is input directly into the mixer, he can listen to the tracks over external speakers.

An overdub may consist of a single track being recorded individually or several simultaneously—it depends on what is being recorded, how many tracks are free, and other criteria.

Why do musicians overdub instead of recording all at once? There are many reasons. It allows fewer people to make a recording; many musicians play several instruments and overdubbing allows one person to record several parts one at a time. Overdubbing is economical in terms of renting studio space. Studios do not have to be very large to make professional recordings with full sounds. Many (or a few) people can record in a small room (at different times). Overdubbing saves time because it enables corrections to be made without everybody having to start from scratch. Without overdubbing for an ensemble recording, one person's mistake would force everyone to begin again. Overdubbing also allows for greater control over each instrument or voice. Without overdubbing, sounds from one recordist could 'leak' into other recordists' microphones. (Sometimes musicians record together—rhythm sections, for instance—and the individuals are separated by 'baffles' or in isolation booths to minimize leakage.)

In overdubbing, the parts to be laid down and the order in which they are to be recorded are a matter of arrangement and personal preference. Here is one example of the kind of overdubs that may be recorded (on top of the basic tracks), and the order in which they might be laid down:

1. Guide vocal
2. Lead parts such as instrumental solos
3. The so-called 'sweeteners,' including strings, horns, and other orchestral instruments
4. Background vocals (group vocals, harmonies)
5. Special effects, such as an explosion or cymbal crash or synthesizer sweep
6. Lead vocal

During recording, the engineer writes on a 'track sheet' which instruments and voices are recording on which particular tracks. This is helpful for both recording and mixing, and reduces the likelihood of accidentally erasing tracks.

Microphone set-up

The set-up of the microphones is important, particularly with regard to acoustic drums and pianos. For master recordings, the number of 'mics' on the acoustic drums could be as few as two, but would more likely be anywhere from seven to 12. A typical drum set consists of a kick drum, snare drum, hi tom tom, mid tom tom, low tom, cymbals, and hi hat. Each of these individual parts could be mic'd individually; again, individual preferences would determine this. Each microphone line goes to a separate channel on the mixing console, which might or might not lead to a different track (this would be the producer's or engineer's decision). For a demo, perhaps only one mic would be used on acoustic drums.

Two microphones are often used to record acoustic pianos—one is placed by the low notes, the other by the high notes. Thus the piano would be recorded in stereo, which, of course, gives aural dimension.

Another consideration in recording these and other acoustic instruments is how far the microphone is placed from the sound source. The distance between the microphone and the sound source affects the way the sound is recorded.

Bouncing

When making demos on a home multitrack tape recorder, you will be 'bouncing.' Bouncing is the process of merging existing tracks to make more room for additional overdubs. For example, if an 8-track recorder is being used and there are many different parts to record, you may, after a number have been recorded, bounce them all onto a single track, leaving the other tracks free for new parts to be recorded. This process can continue, enabling you to record still further new tracks. When you bounce, however, you are fixing the relationship of the parts that are being bounced, and the levels cannot be adjusted later. After all, the tracks have been filled; they are mixed.

Now let's consider a practical example of how bouncing works. If you have an 8-track tape recorder, you can begin by recording on the first six tracks. Then you bounce these all onto track eight. Next you record on tracks one to five. These are bounced to track seven.

Then you record on the first four tracks. You bounce these to track six. Next you record on the first three tracks. These are bounced to track five. Then you record on tracks one and two and bounce these to track four. Finally, you record parts on the first three tracks. Your eight tracks are now filled up, and you mix everything to a 2-track tape which becomes your master from which to make demo copies.

For best results, do not bounce to adjacent tracks. In other words, don't bounce tracks one to five onto track six. Bounce them onto track seven (or eight). But to get the parts down that you want using a 4-track cassette tape recorder, you probably will have to bounce to adjacent tracks. You'll record on the first three, for instance, and bounce them over onto track four. (See chart, page 94.) This cannot be helped, and for the purposes of demoing a song, the audio quality will be sufficient. Don't overdo bouncing; it ultimately results in poorer sound quality, because each bounce is another generation of sound that takes away from the original frequency response. Thus the more you bounce, the less bright the sound will be. Experimentation will guide you. And remember, you can't mix the sounds (instruments or voices) on one track after they have been bounced to that track, because once the sounds are mixed to one track, they cannot be separated.

The recording or mixing console

In multitrack recording, sounds (or signals) travel through a machine called a recording console or mixing console before being stored on tape or before reaching the speakers during playback. The machine, which processes and routes signals, is called by either name because it functions in both recording and mixing. More information about consoles appears in Chapter Three.

Signal flow

In the 'live' recording process, sounds are made (by instruments, voices or both), stored on tape, and listened back to through speakers. For the devices involved, recording consists of taking energy in one form (sound), converting it to another (electrical).

storing it on tape in another form again (magnetic), and then reversing the process so that the energy is ultimately reconverted to its original, audible form, acoustical energy. Specifically, then, what is the flow of the signal in recording?

Sound emanates from a source—in recording, a singer or a musician. A person performs a part into a microphone (except when recording with an electronic instrument by direct input; we'll keep to tracing the signal flow by using the microphone as our starting point). The microphone is the first of a series of 'transducers' in the recording system. A transducer is a device that changes one form of energy to another. A microphone converts acoustical energy (the movement of air molecules) into electrical energy. When acoustical energy hits the microphone, the mic puts out an electrical signal that needs to be boosted or cut. The signal travels to the recording console, where a preamplifier raises or reduces the signal as needed.

Once in the console, the signal can be processed. (Equalization and reverb, for example, are two types of signal processors.) Next, the electronic signal travels from the console to the multitrack tape recorder, where it magnetizes the tape (see the section 'How Sound Is Recorded onto Magnetic Tape').

The preceding discussion explains how signals travel from sound source to tape. After the information has been recorded, it is played back. The playing back of signals is the system in reverse (except that the end point is a speaker, of course, instead of a microphone). The signals, stored as magnetic energy on the tape (now a permanent magnet), are converted into electrical energy. They travel from the tape recorder to the mixing console to a power amp (where they are boosted) and finally to the speakers, which emit acoustical energy or sound.

Figs. 2—4 show signal flow in the various stages of the recording process: basic tracks, overdubs, and mixing, respectively.

Fig. 2 SIGNAL FLOW IN RECORDING OF BASIC TRACKS

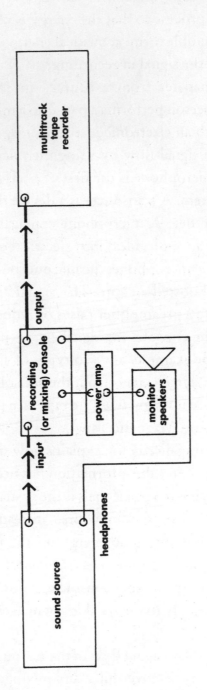

In recording the basic tracks, the signal travels from the sound source, to the mixing console, and from there to the multitrack tape recorder. The sound is heard in the control room on monitor speakers, and the musician in the studio hears a mix on headphones.

Fig. 3 SIGNAL FLOW IN OVERDUBS

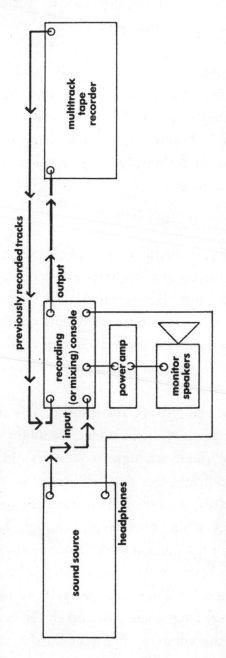

In recording the overdub, the previously recorded tracks are fed from the multitrack tape recorder to the mixing console so the musician in the studio and the engineer and producer in the control room may hear new parts being recorded in conjunction with the previous tracks.

Fig. 4 SIGNAL FLOW DURING MIXING

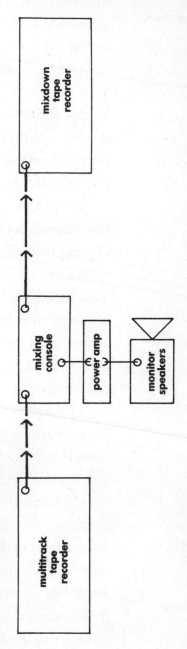

In the mixdown, the signals recorded on multitrack tape are passed through the mixing console, where they are blended at different levels, and then recorded on two tracks, or stereo tape.

Diagrams by John Barilla, Randy Battiste, and David Copper.

Signal enhancement

In multitrack recording and mixing, sound is enhanced by various electronic effects. Among these are equalization, filtering, reverb and delay.

These effects are used on all 'pop' records made today, and you need only hear how these same records would sound without them to appreciate what a difference they can make! When recording and mixing multitrack demos, you (or your engineer) will be using electronic effects. Understanding what they are and how they work can only serve to improve your demos.

Equalization and filtering

During recording and mixing, it is sometimes desirable to boost or eliminate certain frequencies, resulting in a brighter or duller sound. This process is known as 'equalization' (abbreviated to EQ), and is accomplished by the use of an 'equalizer' in the recording console. An engineer can use an equalizer to enhance or reduce frequencies in the low, mid and high ranges, or use its filter to 'roll off' or eliminate frequencies.

During recording, a musician might ask for more or less in a given frequency range. In studio jargon, for instance, he might say something like "Add more top" (ie, more high frequencies). High frequencies are responsible for brightness and brilliance, so this would mean the person wanted the sound of his instrument to be brighter. (Note, however, that while not having enough high frequencies makes the sound muffled, an excessive amount sounds shrill.) If a musician asked for a sound to be 'fattened up' a bit, he would be referring to low frequencies. Thus an engineer would add low frequencies or low mid-range frequencies. If a producer says a sound needs more 'presence,' the engineer might boost the mid-range area.

These changes may all be made using controls on the recording console. Once you hear for yourself how manipulating frequencies affects the sound of your demo, you'll be able to enhance your song by requesting these applications as a musician in the studio, or by effecting them yourself on your home multitrack system.

Reverb

A popular form of sound enhancement in recording (particularly of vocals) is 'reverberation,' or reverb, It is usually not used in recording the basic tracks but is added later, during the mix. This is because it is very difficult while recording to ascertain how much reverb will be needed. Some musicians like to hear reverb in the monitor mix because they want to hear what the sound wth reverb will be like later. To make the musicians more at ease, the engineer might put a certain amount of reverb into a monitor mix without actually recording the effect.

A reverberation unit creates multiple echoes that build up to a certain density and appear to sound randomly from all around the listener; the summation of the echoes is reverberation. A reverberation unit simulates the summation of all the echoes in an acoustical environment, to create an effect of lengthening of the sound (as if you were recording or performing in a much bigger area than you actually are).

Delay lines

An effective way to enhance sounds during recording and mixing is to create a time lag of audio signals, which results in the simulation of echoes and other special effects. This is achieved by the use of devices referred to as 'delay lines.'

Delay lines may be set to delay signals at different time intervals. Different delay times will give effects known as flanging, chorusing, doubling, slapback echo, short echo, and long echo. They are applied to the instruments and voices that have been recorded or are being played live, giving new dimension to that particular sound.

Using effects to embellish sounds can be just as creative a process as coming up with parts for the recording. There are no rules

Note: Delay
units include
other parameters
besides delay
time that can
contribute to the
final effect.
Feedback control,
for example,
determines how
many repeats the
echo will have.
The time delays
given are
approximate, and
subject to the
user's discretion.

Effects can
be best
understood
through hearing
them. If you do
not own signal
processing
equipment, ask
for a
demonstration in
a music shop.
Better still, if
someone you
know has the
equipment,
perhaps he or she
will be able to
spend some time
showing you the
effects that can be
achieved and
how to create
them.

governing which effects are to be applied to particular instruments and voices or for certain types of songs. It's a matter of personal taste. If you have signal processing equipment at home, you'll experiment and eventually get a sense of what effect to use when. If you record in a commercial studio, the engineer will use his own judgement and ask your opinion. If he doesn't, tell him to. Rather than just saying "Yes, I like that" or "No, that's not the sound I want," you should become familiar with exactly what it is that he is doing to create that effect.

The various types of delay line are illustrated in the following table. A more complete discussion of the effects follows the table.

NAME OF EFFECT	APPROXIMATE TIME DELAY RANGE ON THE UNIT	EFFECT CREATED
flanging	1 millisecond (ms) to 10 ms	a swishing, sweeping phasing effect like a jet plane. Use it when you want to give the effect of sound rushing to and away from the listener in pulses
chorusing	10 ms to 45 ms	gives a fatter sound like a layering of two sounds at once
doubling	45 ms to 100 ms	the effect is similar to chorusing, but since a longer delay time is at work, the listener can distinguish two independent sounds
slapback echo	100 ms to 145 ms	a quick, one-shot repeat of a sound that gives, as its name suggests, a 'slapback' effect
short echo	145 ms to 300 ms	two or three repeats of a short musical phrase
long echo	300 ms to 2 seconds	the repeating of an entire musical phrase (the length of the phrase determines how many times it repeats)

Echoes are the most basic effect that may be created by a delay line. An echo is a single slap or reflection of a sound. Multiple reflections of a sound (echoes of an echo) are another effect. Delay lines can simulate multiple reflections by what is called 'feedback' or 'resonance' control.

Other effects that may be obtained by a delay line are: flanging, doubling, chorusing, slapback echoes and long delay. All of these effects are variations in the range of delay times that may be set by the engineer. The delays commonly range from 1 ms to 1 second; some high-quality delay lines extend to up to 5 seconds or more (usually these extra long delay times are used for broadcast purposes rather than for recording songs).

Flanging is a phase cancellation effect where certain frequencies are removed, resulting in a swirling jet-plane effect. This is achieved by very short delay times, ranging from 1 to 10 ms, and a certain amount of feedback (a potentiometer feeds the signal back into the circuit at a lesser level than the input signal, where it travels in a loop and eventually dies out).

Doubling simulates the double performance of a part by adding slight time differences that give a realistic effect. The signal is delayed within the range of 15 ms to 60 ms with a certain amount of 'modulation' (modulation means an automatic varying of the delay time above and below the indicated point). Doubling is often used to simulate one person singing along with himself. The process is sometimes called artificial double tracking (ADT). It should be noted that the ear cannot 'resolve' (distinguish) a repeat unless it is at least 30 ms behind. The sound appears to fuse, with the result being a 'fattened' or thickened sound, but no discrete echo can be discerned.

Chorusing simulates multiple replications of a sound by creating a group effect. A group singing will most certainly exhibit 'errors' in exact performance, giving the characteristic 'choral' sound. The 'errors' will result in cancellation of sound that changes over time. It is somewhere between the 'sweepy' sound of flanging and the fatness of doubling, about 7 to 15 ms. As with doubling, a certain amount of modulation is added. The voice of a single individual, or even the sound of a single instrument, can be chorused to give the impression of an ensemble sound.

Slapback echo is a discrete echo of short duration. It is effected by delaying a signal within the range of 60 to 200 ms. By using feedback, the amount of echo will be increased (that is, there will be more repeats before the sound dies out).

Long delay is a discrete echo of long duration. The signal is delayed within the range of 200 ms to about 2 seconds. When regeneration (or feedback) is added, the sound becomes very 'ambient', like that produced by a performance in a large, resonant hall. With long echoes (and sometimes short echoes as well), it is often beneficial to set the timing of the delay so that the echoes beat rhythmically with the tempo of the song.

Mixing

After all the tracks of a multitrack recording have been recorded, there is separately stored information on four, eight, or however many tracks of the multitrack tape have been used. It is necessary at this point to blend all the separately recorded sounds into a final product. This is the stage called *mixing*.

Mixing, or mixdown, results in a stereo, or 2-track recording, which may be used for making copies (such as for demo purposes), or for mastering a record, compact disc or tape. During the mixdown a number of adjustments are made: the volumes of the recorded parts are adjusted relative to one another; signals are processed with equalization; the sounds of certain parts are modified by outboard signal processors to give them a particular texture, quality or special effect; the instruments and vocals are placed in a stereo panorama; and the overall ambience of the recording may be embellished with the use of reverb.

Mixing provides a second opportunity to manipulate sounds that have been previously recorded. What was technically input during recording—equalization and signal processing—may be superimposed again. These effects may be added not only to the individual tracks but also to the summation of all the tracks. For example, reverb can be added to the final mix to create the impression of a uniform ambience—that is, the impression that everybody recorded in the same room at the same time.

Dynamics and panning

Dynamics may be added to the mix where there were previously none. Dynamics may not have originally been recorded because you recorded for the optimum level of the signal on tape. But in the mixdown, you can put some life into the recording. Dynamics are added by means of the 'fader,' a device that lets you 'ride' the tracks, putting in effects such as crescendos and diminuendos.

During mixing, the recorded sounds can be distributed over the stereo spectrum so that they have a position in the panorama. This is effected with a knob called the 'pan pot' on the mixing console, and the process is called 'panning.' The pan pot allows you to place a single sound anywhere in the left to right spectrum.

In the mixdown process, single sounds can be transformed into artificial stereo. For example, a delay line can be used to slightly delay the sound of a single guitar part and create a double track of the part. The real guitar part can then be put on the left side and the artificially delayed sound on the right side to give the effect of two guitarists playing at the same time, one on the left side of the room and the other on the right side.

There are no rules for the placement of sounds for a stereo perspective; it's a matter of personal taste and popular convention. Fig. 5 shows sample distribution of instruments and voices.

Whereas panning creates *breadth* of field, left to right (stereo), reverb can be used to create *depth* of field, front to back. The less reverb there is on a signal, the closer to the listener the sound appears (because there are few reflections of sound); the more reverb, the

Fig. 5 DISTRIBUTION OF INSTRUMENTS AND VOICES IN THE STEREO SPECTRUM

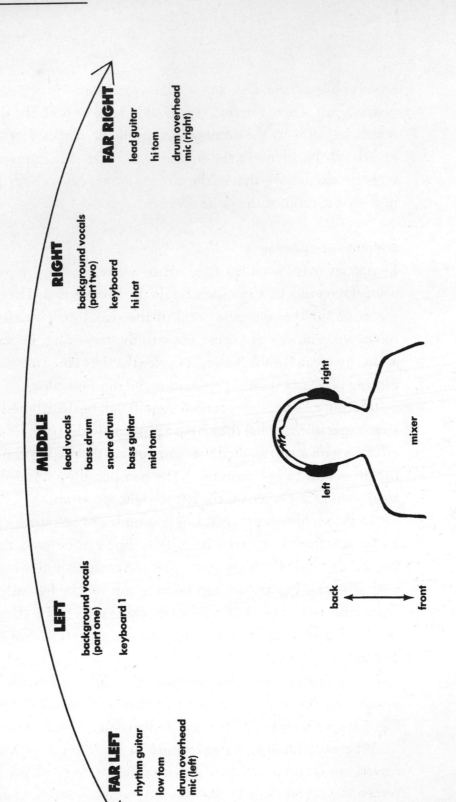

FAR LEFT

rhythm guitar

low tom

drum overhead
mic (left)

LEFT

background vocals
(part one)

keyboard 1

MIDDLE

lead vocals

bass drum

snare drum

bass guitar

mid tom

RIGHT

background vocals
(part two)

keyboard

hi hat

FAR RIGHT

lead guitar

hi tom

drum overhead
mic (right)

back

front

left

right

mixer

Virtual tracks are created through artificial doubling with a delay line. There is only one actual performance, but in the mix it will appear as two. This is a great way to save track space, but still gets stereo imaging.

further away the sound appears (because there are more reflections of sound). With the use of reverb, you can create the perspective, for example, of the lead singer right in front of the listener and the backing singers standing behind the lead vocalist.

How mixing works

Each person may have his or her own way of mixing but a simple, generalized explanation of the process for songs is as follows:

The mixer studies the track sheet that was compiled during the recording process. This tells what instruments and vocals are on which particular tracks. The multitrack tape is placed on the tape recorder. A piece of masking tape is placed in front of the entire array of faders on the mixing console. Each individual track is now labelled on the masking tape.

The mixer listens to each of the individual tracks and analyzes what has been recorded. He might make a rough mix to get the basic levels of all the parts, to get a feel for the song, and to familiarize himself as to how long the parts last and what the tracks are all about. Having done this, he goes to the very beginning, to the rhythm tracks, to work with each track closely and to obtain a very careful blend of the instruments.

Mixers often start with the drums. Some prefer to go from the lowest to the highest; in this instance, the kick drum is processed first. To get a satisfactory sound, the mixer might use equalization delay, reverb, compression, or any other electronic effect he deems necessary to get the sound he's looking for. These may all be used simultaneously to get that certain 'sock' desired out of the kick drum. Following this, the mixer would go to the snare (on which he repeats the process), and then to the other pieces of the drum set in order to get everything balanced.

Next, the mixer equalizes and signal-processes the bass with the drums. Equalizing, signal processing and perhaps other processes (such as artificial double tracking) are done next with the midrange instruments (keyboards, guitars), followed by other instrumental overdubs. Following this, the vocals might be mixed, and reverb might be added to the vocals. After this, solo instrumental overdubs might be mixed. The mixer tries to get the solo to complement—that is, enhance but not overshadow—the lead vocal. Finally, special effects might be mixed into the overall sound, and any final adjustments made. The levels from the mixdown tape recorder are adjusted, and the mix is transferred to a 2-track tape recorder. The 2-track stereo tape that you make becomes your new master from which you make copies. It should also be mentioned that computers may be used to control the mix. The computer remembers all the levels and effects and calls them up as they are needed. This process is known as 'automated mixing.'

The human ear is most sensitive to mid-range audio levels. At moderate listening levels, the ear is much less sensitive to both low frequency signals and high frequency signals, but as the volume of a sound is raised in the studio, the ear becomes increasingly sensitive to the lows and highs. If you are monitoring a mix at a very high volume, then you would hear a lot of lows and highs in addition to the mid-range sounds, which might sound terrific. But if the mix is taken out of the studio and played at a low level on a typical cassette player or car stereo, the listener might find it deficient in the lows and highs.

On the other hand, if you mix at a very low volume, you might find an excess of lows and highs when the tape is played back at a high volume. In general, then, it's best to mix at a moderate level. However, if there is a special application for the recording, adjust the monitor level accordingly. For example, a dance recording might be mixed at a very high level, an easy listening tune at a low level.

It's important to listen to your mix on different size speakers— big and little—before printing a final version. This will help ensure that the mix will sound good on any speaker system and at any volume. For instance, large speakers will give a tremendous bass response but little ones will not, so you need to choose a bass frequency that will cut through properly on all speakers.

Remember, mixing is important, but there is no need to be obsessed with it. Demos are not expected to be finished master recordings. Rather, they serve to present songs in a favourable way, still leaving room for the imagination to take a song to even greater heights.

Multitrack recording and mixing are complicated, but don't be intimidated by these processes. You'll learn them by experimenting, and once you get the hang of it, a world of great demo recording will open up for you, where you're the boss!

CHAPTER THREE

THE RECORDING STUDIO

There are different kinds of recording studios to accommodate the needs of songwriters, musicians and record producers. Commonly, there are 8-track, 16-track, 24-track, 48-track and 64-track studios. What this means is that the studios have a multitrack tape recorder capable of recording that many tracks. Many studios have more than one recording room with machines capable of recording fewer tracks than the one in the main room. Time is less expensive in these rooms, and they're often used by songwriters to make demos.

Even if you record at home, it is important for you to understand the set-up of a commercial recording studio—what equipment is there and how everything works—because after all, a home studio is still a studio, only on a smaller scale and with equipment and an acoustical environment that are not as professional. So the more you know about the kinds of equipment available and how to create the right acoustics, the better your demos will be. Many songwriters do record in professional studios instead of investing the same money in home equipment because they prefer the services of a skilled engineer or they just don't want to bother learning how to record and mix on home multitrack equipment. There are other songwriters who are members of groups, and in such cases, the spaciousness of the studio is more conducive to recording than the home. Many of you will be recording your demos in studios, and if you ever cut masters, you inevitably will be recording there too. So for these reasons, this chapter will go into detail on the workings of a professional studio.

What is a recording studio?

The term 'studio' has two meanings. It can refer to an entire commercial facility where recordings are made, including the control room, an office, and other areas. Or it can refer to the particular room where recordings are made by instrumentalists and vocalists, a room separated by a wall and window fron the 'control room' where performances are monitored, controlled electronically, and recorded.

Studios, as rooms where performers record, vary in size, but a studio doesn't have to be huge for mastering pop records. Remember, the musicians and singers do not record their parts all at once but in separate sessions, beginning with the basic tracks and followed by the various overdubs.

If you were to make a demo at a studio, you would probably use a smaller room, if there were more than one. This would adequately suit your purposes and you wouldn't have to worry about your demo having less quality than one recorded in the main studio. You just don't need all that space, and it's much more expensive.

Studios are wonderful places for songwriters. It is there that your songs finally come to life in a grand way. You end up with a tape that was professionally recorded and one that you needn't be ashamed to play to anyone. Of course, quality tapes may be obtained from home recording, but in addition to getting the benefit of expert equipment and engineering in the studio, there is one other advantage that you may not get when recording at home—the energy or excitement that you may get from working in a studio. You live at home, so it's often difficult to get inspired performances, but in the studio, when the lights are dim and you're sitting before a microphone with the engineer and anyone else in the control room looking out at you through the glass window, you might feel a certain spark that causes you to perform superbly.

Equipment and instruments

What equipment or instruments do you have to bring to the studio? What will they provide? Studios vary widely, but for recording, they should all supply at least the following:

- multitrack tape recorder
- mixdown tape recorder (stereo)
- mixing desk
- outboard gear (good selection)
- monitoring equipment
- microphones (good selection)
- headphones
- tape

Studios may or may not be equipped with sequencers, synthesizers, samplers, expanders, drum machines, and other instruments such as acoustic and electric pianos, acoustic and electronic drum kits, and so on. What they don't have, they can hire in for you, but, once again, check the rates first.

How to choose a studio

If you decide to record in a professional studio, there may be several in your area from which you may choose, Of course, studios in a particular area may be inconveniently located, so geography is still a consideration.

There are several other factors to weigh in selecting a studio. At the top are rates. Comparable studios in the same area may vary widely in the prices they charge. Investigate them and ask for rate cards. Examine rates for both recording and mixing, as well as for material (tape) costs.

Then consider value for money. How many tracks do you get to use? Two studios may have the same hourly rate, but one studio may have a 16-track machine while the other one has only an 8-track. Find out if the rates are cheaper at a certain time of the day or if the studio will let you record at a less expensive rate when they have 'down time' (that is, when no one is booked to record). Don't be afraid to negotiate. Any customer is better than none, and studios don't want to lose your business.

Ask what instruments and equipment they supply, and which ones you have to provide yourself or rent. You might find also that studios vary widely in this respect.

Check into the availability of the studio for the times you want. You might decide on a certain studio and find that they are booked solid over the next few months for the times in which you can record. Chances are they'll probably have the studio open for a time that is convenient to you.

Another important consideration is friendliness. Meet the engineer. Discuss your project before you go in to record, if you can. Size him up not only for his technical expertise and creativity (whatever you may be able to gather in a short meeting), but also for his personality. Is he someone with whom you feel you could get along during your session and who can help you, tell you your options, and do the best job for your song? An engineer isn't simply someone who pushes buttons. He's the technical pilot for your session, and he can suggest routes to make the cruise more eventful and productive.

Some studios will get you an arranger, producer, musicians or singers if you need them. For many songwriters, this can be an extremely valuable service, and you should inquire as to whether the studios can recommend people who can help you make your demo.

You can also ask how the equipment is maintained. Chances are they'll service the equipment on a regular basis, and if they don't, they wouldn't tell you anyway!

Find out what kinds of equipment the studios have. It might be interesting to compare the answers from various studios. Are there computers and sequencers for recording? If you did pre-production by MIDI at home, can you bring in your instruments to transfer the data to multitrack tape?

What kinds of outboard gear—that is, reverberation units, noise/gate expanders, and other signal processors—does the studio have?

Most will have a full range of these, but if you're recording in a cheap studio, it's important to know that these are available.

You might also inquire about the studio's lighting system. Psychologically and emotionally, many artists perform better in an environment that allows them to let down all inhibitions or that inspires them in some way. To create particular moods and meet the needs of singers and musicians, studios have lighting systems that provide a variety of effects, including different colours. A darkened studio, for example, may stimulate the feeling of being on stage in front of a live audience. Find out what the studio has in the way of lighting.

Last but not least is the quality of the studio itself. As a non-expert, it will be difficult for you to make a judgement (it would even be difficult for a pro by just looking around), but there are things for you to be aware of, and you can ask questions. Is the equipment up to date? Is it state-of-the-art? What are the acoustics like? We'll get to these shortly.

It should be said that there are subjective criteria for you to consider. Word of mouth is one. Do you have any friends who have recorded at the studios that you are thinking of using? Get their feedback and listen to their tapes. In fact, you should ask the studio people if you can hear a sample of a recording made at their facility.

Is the studio appealing to you? Does it have a nice appearance and is it clean, or do you find it filthy and not kept up well. This may or may not necessarily relate to the quality of the studio, but it may have a psychological effect on you.

There are studios on commercial property and studios set up in houses. Don't overlook the latter. Just because someone has a studio in a basement or a bedroom doesn't mean that you can't get a recording there as good as one from a studio in a building. The rates may be cheaper, and you might find the owner more eager to help you and willing to provide services that you wouldn't get elsewhere.

But again, you need to investigate the quality of the equipment and the acoustics.

Equipment

There are two factors that determine the quality of equipment—multitrack tape recorders, mixing boards and so forth: how well it was constructed—what kinds of parts, what special features, and what craftsmanship went into it—and how well it is maintained. Of course, how well it is operated will also influence its quality. To help you learn more about equipment, read magazines and ask around. Find out how the different brands differ, and how this might affect you. Actually, for demo purposes, any professional equipment should suffice, but as you become more knowledgeable about equipment, this will probably translate into making better demos.

Acoustics

Acoustics are an important consideration when choosing a studio to record in. Great equipment is not used to its maximum effectiveness if the acoustics of the studio have not been constructed and designed well. In general, studios are designed, with respect to both shape and materials, to get excellent quality sound. In fact, many studios are designed by individuals who are experts in the science of acoustics.

In multitrack pop recording, every attempt is made to keep each track as pure as possible—to capture only the sound(s) of the source(s) being recorded, to separate the elements rather than record them as an ensemble. In this way, the integrity of each individual sound source can be faithfully reproduced later, and mixed and processed with outboard gear as desired. This is affected not only by the design and materials of the studio, but also by the recording techniques and equipment used. For example, microphones able to discriminate sounds coming from sources other than the singer or musician are commonly used. The selection of proper mics is vital in recording the rhythm section—piano, bass, guitar, and drums—for the basic tracks, where the goal is to minimize leakage. How they are placed spacially in relation to the sound source is also important, as microphones have different pickup patterns (see Chapter Seven, 'Home Recording').

'Live' vs. 'Dead.' Acoustically, professional studios may be considered to be characterized by two different types of areas: a 'dead' (or 'dry') end and a 'live' (or 'wet') end. A dead end has soft, absorbent surfaces. It contains padded material that absorbs reflections of sound. Typically, electronic instruments are recorded in dry areas. A live end has hard, reflective surfaces. It may be made of dense wood, such as oak or teak; cement blocks covered with ceramic tile; or other materials that tend to bounce sounds so as to capture the ambience of a spacious room, such as a large hall. Orchestral instruments, such as violins, oboes and clarinets, are often recorded in wet areas.

Sometimes, panels or portable walls set on castors, called baffles, are used to create different acoustical ambiences. A baffle made of beech wood, for example, would have a hard, reflective surface on one side, while the other side could be covered with fibreglass and fabric to make it absorbent. In effect, one side of the baffle is live, the other side dead. Depending on the ambience desired, the engineer would use one side or the other. For example, if a guitarist were recording, the engineer might face the guitarist's amplifier toward the absorbent side of the baffle and place a microphone near the amplifier's speaker.

Not all instruments record with microphones facing amplifiers. Electric instruments (such as a guitar) and electronic instruments (such as a synthesizer) may record by direct input, in which signals travel directly though wire and an amplifier is not used. (No sound is heard unless a listener is using headphones or is in the control room.) It is not always desirable to record by direct input, however, for there is a certain coloration of sound when it hits air, and this may be desired.

OTHER ACOUSTIC FEATURES

Acoustically designed studios may not have parallel walls. With parallel walls, sound travels back and forth and is reinforced, creating 'standing waves'. They give a room a particular characteristic or tonal quality, no matter what sound is emitted. Coloration of a room, acoustically, should be avoided. A studio should be as neutral as possible, and should not have a characteristic 'sound.' Thus the studio may have some irregular or unusual form, such as an octagonal shape. Because corners also tend to reinforce sound, the area where walls meet may be rounded. In some studios, the ceiling may slope, again to help minimize reflections of sound.

Separating the studio from the control room is a wall containing a window through which people in the control room and the studio can see each other. There may be a door built into the wall for people to move back and forth between the rooms, or there may be doors for people to enter and exit on the sides of both the studio and the control room. Between the studio and control rooms are wires that form the electrical connection between the rooms. These may be threaded through metal pipes to shield against magnetic induction.

Although the studio and control room are adjoining, there should be as much acoustical independence or separation between the two as possible. Acoustical energy is transmitted through walls, which act as conducting mediums.

The people in the control room, who will be evaluating and perhaps colouring the sounds as they are played, should hear the sounds as purely as possible. They need to hear the sounds being generated in the studio only through the monitor speakers and not in any way through the wall. They should not even hear or feel any vibrations. Acoustic designers go to great lengths to keep each room acoustically separate and to prevent 'leakage.' Some even build the adjoining wall with concrete, extending it down to the earth so sound will not be conducted through other materials.

The acoustic design of the doors is also a matter of concern, since they may act as conductors of sound. Some are lined with lead, and weigh hundreds of pounds.

The glass window may actually be two or three panes in thickness. The panes may not be set parallel, but at angles to each other, to prevent the build-up of significant resonance. The thickness and angular design of the glass will prevent or minimize vibrations, such as those caused by the playing of a bass guitar, from passing through to the control room.

The control room

The control room is the area where you (as producer of your demos) will monitor, evaluate and direct performances, and where the engineer operates the recording, mixing and signal processing equipment. It is considered the centre of the entire studio complex, because it is where sounds—indeed, the actual overall recording of a song—can, as the room's name implies, be controlled—modified, balanced, coloured and embellished.

Equipment and devices

Typically, a control room will contain the following equipment:

1. Mixing console. All electrical signals pass through and are processed in a large desk-like board called the recording (or mixing) console.
2. Recording equipment. There are various types and configurations of machines that fall under this heading:
   a. analogue multitrack tape recorder. This may be a 16-track, 24-track, or 32-track machine, and two tape recorders can be 'locked together' in synchronization to provide more tracks.
   b. digital multitrack tape recorder.
3. Mixdown tape recorder. When the multitrack tape is being mixed, the sounds will be transferred to another tape recorder. The mixdown machine will record the final, stereo recording.

4. Noise reduction equipment. This may be built into a tape recorder or be a separate unit. It helps eliminate extraneous noise (like tape hiss) that builds up when recording.

5. Patch bay. This unit is a sort of switchboard for studio wiring. Instead of all the cables from the studio feeding directly into the mixing console, they go into the patch bay, or patch panel, which makes connecting things easier and expedites signal routing and processing.

6. Outboard gear. This term refers to signal processing devices that create special effects: compressor/limiters, which allow a vocal or instrumental part to be recorded at a consistent level (the compressor function) and control the dynamic ranges of loud and soft passages being recorded (the limiter function); noise gates, which keep out unwanted sound during recording; reverb units, which simulate different types of room sound; and delay units, which create the effects of flanging, chorusing, doubling, slapback echo, short echo and long echo (discussed in Chapter Two, 'Multitrack Recording and Mixing').

7. Sequencer. A sequencer records and plays back MIDI data (see Chapter Five, 'MIDI'). Sequencers can come in hardware form—that is, as separate, stand-alone, 'dedicated' units—or as computer software.

8. Computers and computer software (see Chapter Seven, 'Home Recording').

9. Power amplifiers.

10. Monitors. There will be a minimum of two monitor speakers in the control room, and probably several sets of different sizes, so that you can get an idea of what a mix will sound like on the various kinds of speakers that people have.

Speakers are made in a variety of ways. A three-way speaker consists of a 'woofer', a mid-range speaker and a 'tweeter'. A two-way speaker has a woofer and a tweeter. A one-way speaker contains only a woofer. Woofers bring out the low frequencies of sound, mid-range speakers the upper end of the low frequency range to the lower end of the high frequency range, and tweeters the high frequencies of sound.

Mixing consoles

The mixing console (or mixer, recording console or board) is the 'central switchboard' of the recording process. It contains many knobs, buttons, switches and faders that can be used to change the timbre, volume and location of sound being recorded and mixed, as well as perform various other functions. It enables the engineer to control the audio signals that are fed into it.

As mentioned, the mixer is located in the control room. Connected to it are microphone lines and direct line inputs from instruments in the studio. Audio signals come into the console, are boosted or cut by a preamp, and may then be manipulated by the engineer. The signals flow from the mixer's output to the multitrack tape recorder's input, where they travel to the heads and are stored on tape. The signals travel again from the tape deck's output to inputs of the mixer for processing during overdubbing or mixing. The board can also enable people to hear a separate monitor mix in the control room (which is not necessarily the mix that is being recorded) or give a separate mix to musicians in the studio (called a cue or headphone mix), or be used for equalization.

Multitrack tape recorders

A multitrack tape recorder is one that can record two or more tracks onto tape. The following table lists the types of multitrack tape recorder and the width of recording tape they use:

MULTITRACK TAPE RECORDER (ANALOGUE)	WIDTH TAPE USED
2-track reel-to-reel	$1/4$ inch, $1/2$ inch
2-track cassette	$1/8$ inch (standard cassette width)
4-track reel-to-reel	$1/4$ inch, $1/2$ inch
4-track cassette	$1/4$ inch, $1/2$ inch, 1 inch
8-track reel-to-reel	$1/8$ inch
8-track cassette	$1/8$ inch, $1/2$ inch
16-track reel-to-reel	1 inch, 2 inch
24-track reel-to-reel	2 inch
32-track reel-to-reel	2 inch

Demos are commonly made on 2-, 4-, 8-, or 16-track machines. Masters are usually made on 16-, 24-, or 32-track machines, or with more tracks by the 'lock-up' of machines.

Tapes with bigger widths are used in recording a greater number of tracks because more information (tracks) can be stored on them. Open-reel (or reel-to-reel) tape recorders move at speeds of 17/8 inches per second (ips), $3^3/4$ ips, $7^1/2$ ips, 15 ips, and 30 ips. The faster the tape moves, the cleaner the sound that will be recorded.

Professional tape recorders have three heads: the erase head, the record/sync head and the playback head. The erase head does only what its name says: it erases information recorded onto a tape. The record/sync head performs the dual functions of recording and playing back and is necessary for overdubbing. The playback head is used when mixing.

Maintenance of the tape recorder is vital. In a recording studio, bias and azimuth adjustments are set to reference tones on tape in every session to ensure that the frequencies and tones are recorded accurately. The heads may be cleaned several times per day. Failure to clean the heads can result in 'dropouts' (audibly noticeable diminutions of recorded sound). All other parts in the tape path are cleaned also: the guides, lifters, capstan and pinch roller. Demagnetization is also performed to cancel out build-up of permanent magnetic fields on the ferric parts of the tape recorder. Unless neutralized, magnetic fields can result in tics, pops, poor high frequency response and other aberrations.

Acoustics

As with the studio, the acoustics of the control room are of vital importance. Because sounds will be evaluated here for recording and mixing, it is desirable to have as neutral a room as possible, one where tones will not be coloured when they are heard.

The recording engineer

In general, the engineer may be described as one who shapes sounds that are being recorded by manipulating the flow of energy. There is a tendency to think of the engineer as a technician who just operates equipment. This couldn't be further from the truth. By way of comparison to film-making, the recording engineer's job is analogous to those of the cameraman, lighting operator, mixer and film editor. The engineer performs a multitude of tasks in the pre-production, recording, mixing, and editing stages of making a demo or a master.

Responsibilities of the engineer include setting up and testing the tape recorders, selecting microphones, testing lines, getting sound levels, equalizing, working with the outboard gear to create a lively monitor mix for musicians in the studio and the producer (or client) in the control room, and keeping a track sheet. Often the engineer will have an assistant to perform various tasks, including setting up and operating the tape recorders. During sessions, the engineer interprets the qualitative descriptions of sound for the producer and musicians (who might say a sound is too boxy, puffy, fat or thin) and changes them into quantitative input on the machinery to achieve technically what the participants desire to hear.

A trained engineer will have studied such subjects as acoustic and audio theory; the characteristics of microphones; electricity and electronics; digital electronics; electronic maintenance and repair; the operating principles of mixing consoles, multitrack tape recorders and outboard gear; the techniques of recording, mixing and editing; production techniques and studio design; computer operating; and the business of operating a recording studio. Many engineers do not have any formal training but learned their craft from working in studios in some sort of apprenticeship position. For schooled and unschooled engineers alike, it usually takes years of practical ('hands on') experience to develop the skills (and the intuition) necessary to become truly adept at engineering recording sessions.

Studio expenses The cost of making a demo in a studio varies as much as studios do themselves. After all, studios differ in equipment, personnel, and location. Two 8-track studios would probably have different rates, as would two state-of-the-art studios. In general, the expenses incurred in making a demo at a studio are for recording time, mixing time, tape, rental of equipment and instruments (if needed), and payment to musicians and vocalists (if needed). Request rate cards and compare the prices studios charge for recording, mixing and tapes.

CHAPTER FOUR

MODERN ELECTRONIC MUSICAL INSTRUMENTS

Have you heard? There's a revolution going on and you, the songwriter, are kindly invited to participate. It is a revolution of musical instrument technology (based on computer chips called microprocessors) that has rewritten the rules of the craft of songwriting and has altered the way musicians make, arrange, produce and edit music.

Up until the 1970s, the term 'electric musical instruments' generally referred to electric guitars, organs and pianos. The age of the modern synthesizer, however, ushered in a complex array of new instruments and related equipment that could barely have even been conceived of but a few years earlier.

Electronic musical instruments of what we shall call the computer era—digital synthesizers, drum machines, sequencers, samplers and much more— are used in recording both demos and masters, as well as in live (concert) performances. As a songwriter you should be familiar with these instruments, not just because they might enhance your recordings, but because even without playing experience or previous use, you can learn to operate them well enough to do your own demos. Then they'll play an important role in your musical creations.

Indeed, electronic musical instruments can open up a whole new world of music for you. You can create a variety of sounds and rhythms and record and play them back immediately. Your home can become a workshop for you to craft songs or tailor ideas into finished masterpieces! New sounds and rhythms will inspire you to create music that you might not have been able to come up with on your acoustic instrument. It's like going from a conventional typewriter to a word processor. But at all times remember, it ultimately comes down to the song. With whatever you use, your goal (outside of any extraneous personal endeavours) will be to come up with a tune that is catchy, easy to sing, and memorable.

There are various modern electronic musical instruments that are available and of interest to songwriters in writing and making demos. Detailed information on particular models may be obtained from manufacturers and retailers. To keep up with the ever-evolving technology and products, read music magazines and newspapers, attend seminars and conventions, and ask questions of any well informed source.

How electronic instruments may help the songwriter

There are various ways modern electronic musical instruments may help or change the way that songwriters compose.

With synthesizers you can create a myriad of sounds. Each of these sounds will have a certain texture or 'personality,' and you might find yourself creating in a manner that is indicative or suggestive of a particular type of sound. A different sound could influence you to experiment, or to write in a style you haven't previously used. There is also a quality about notes played on an electronic keyboard that differs from those played on acoustic pianos. This too could inspire tunes that might not otherwise have been conceived. Quite simply, a single (and relatively inexpensive) electronic keyboard can provide numerous and varied sounds, and from the songwriter's point of view, there's a lot to be said for that.

'Samplers' enable you to record any sound you like and use it in your music—from your favourite pre-recorded snare drum to a 'live' dog-bark! Samplers can be invaluable creative tools, and this once unaffordable technology is becoming increasingly accessible to home recordists.

Sequencers allow the writer to hear the results of his work immediately. Lay the parts down and push a button, and you can hear everything you've done to that point. No magnetic tape to rewind; the microprocessors do the work instead! Creating new arrangements or editing can also be done right away by pressing the appropriate keys or buttons.

You may also find electronic drum machines a valuable tool for composing. There are three basic types: pre-programmed, programmable, and sampling. The pre-programmed drum machine will enable you to compose melodies on top of a variety of 'stored' rhythms, such as rock, Latin, swing or waltz. You set the kind of rhythm you want and the tempo, and write away! The different types of rhythms should inspire you to come up with lines in the same genre. You may never have even thought about composing a cha-cha or merengue before, but just put on that Latin beat and you'll feel thecreative urge.

Programmable drum machines enable you to create your own rhythmic patterns. You can program any number of styles, tempo changes and time changes that you wish. If you don't want to be limited to the factory-set rhythmic patterns of a pre-programmed drum machine (it can be adjusted in tempo only), the programmable unit may enable you to be more creative in your writing efforts.

Sampling drum machines offer the opportunity for you to program any sound you wish into rhythmic patterns and song formats of your choosing.

Different types of outboard gear can create new ideas and concepts with their special effects. Reverb, digital delays and echo repeats (to name a few) can inspire and spark the songwriter's creative engine.

With the development of modern musical technology, songwriters are interacting with machinery in the creative process as never before. To an expert, the technology influences the writing with the variety of colours, timbres, rhythms, grooves, and 'feels' that may be electronically achieved. Such a writing method differs from the more cerebral processes of composers of yesteryear, but if the results are excellent ... well, how can you knock success?

Overview of musical instruments

The array of modern electronic musical instruments sometimes causes confusion. There are many fancy proprietary names for instruments that do the same thing, and there are also numerous hybrids with the functions of two or more instruments—often known as 'workstations.' To help clarify this, a table of the most common groups of electronic musical instruments follows, as well as a list of conventional instruments whose sounds are simulated by the various synthesizers and drum machines on the market.

As a fine point of distinction, these are actually electric (as opposed to electronic) instruments, since they do not use computer technology

1. Traditional*	2. Synthesizers	3. Samplers	4. Drum Machines	5. Electronic Drum Sets
electric guitar	modular synths: *analogue*	keyboard samplers	pre-programmed	
electric organ			programmable	
electric piano	keyboard synths: *analogue*	sampler modules (expanders)	sampling	
clavinet	*digital/analogue hybrids*			
electric accordion	*FM (digital) additive (digital) synth/sampler hybrids (digital)*	computer-based samplers		
	synth modules (expanders): *(as for keyboard synths)*	sampling drum machines		
	non-keyboard synths: *guitar synths wind synths*			

Conventional (non-electronic) musical instruments

piano (acoustic)	baritone
guitar (acoustic)	trombone
drums (acoustic set)	tuba
accordion	violin
clarinet	viola
flute	cello
piccolo	harp
oboe	double bass
bassoon	bass drum
bass clarinet	snare drum
alto clarinet	cymbals
tenor saxophone	marimba
alto saxophone	tympani
baritone saxophone	chimes
soprano saxophone	wood block
trumpet	bells
cornet	tambourine
French horn	tom tom
English horn	

The conventional instruments listed above are being replaced more and more in pop recording by electronic musical instruments that can not only recreate their sounds, but can also produce a host of others. A detailed examination of their modus operandi is beyond the scope of this book, but now that our interest in these amazing machines is piqued, let's take a closer look at them anyway.

Synthesizers

The synthesizer is a marvel of technology that allows a single person to electronically simulate the sounds of acoustic instruments and of almost anything else. They have evolved tremendously over the years and have been made in various configurations (including guitar, drum and wind synthesizers), but the modern keyboard synthesizer is now universal and quite remarkable.

A keyboard synthesizer can create (synthesize) many different types of sound—sounds of almost any musical instrument, or sounds that might be deemed different, weird, 'new' and even unnatural. It can create non-musical sounds of daily life, such as a dial tone or roaring jet plane. Because of their wide range of possibilities and usefulness (including the economic savings from having to hire many 'live' musicians), synthesizers have become widely accepted in recording (demos and masters), as well as in live performances.

There are two main categories of synthesizer: 'analogue' and 'digital.' Analogue synthesizers are voltage-controlled devices; a change in voltage changes the sound. Digital synthesizers do not use voltage to effect changes in sound. With microprocessors, digital synthesizers use a binary code (consisting of 0s and 1s) as the system to implement or effect commands. Some digital synthesizers are designed with analogue-style controls. Others include sampled sounds that can be layered with synthesized sounds for added realism.

Most keyboards today are designed with touch sensitivity. There are two basic types: 'velocity sensitivity' and 'aftertouch sensitivity.' With velocity sensitivity, the action is analogous to that of the acoustic piano; the keyboard responds dynamically to the touch. With aftertouch (or pressure) sensitivity, the keys respond to pressure applied *after* the initial touch and the result can be programmed to control various parameters (aspects or qualities) of the sound such as volume, filtering (wah wah), vibrato or tremolo.

Most synthesizers have 'pitch-bend' and 'modulation' capability. With pitch-bend, a fundamental tone is bent sharp or flat—that is, raised or lowered—by an assignable or predetermined interval whether it be a perfect fifth, a second, an octave, or any interval in between. The limit of bending of each keyboard is determined by the manufacturer. Depending on the model of the keyboard, pitch-bend can be performed with either a joystick or a pitch wheel. Pitch-bend is generally used for expressive playing, and when properly used can capture the flavour that is characteristic of traditional instruments. A joystick or modulation wheel is used to dial in 'low frequency modulation'. This controls the depth of the vibrato, tremolo and filter-sweeping effects.

Synthesizer modules (expanders)

Synthesizer 'modules,' also referred to as 'expanders,' are essentially synthesizers without the keyboards. Using an expander, you are producing the sounds of an additional keyboard without actually playing it. An expander relies on MIDI (see next chapter) and the use of an external controller (keyboard, guitar or wind) to produce its sounds. Expanders provide the sonic complement to all synthesizers, and because there are no keys to be played, they are generally less expensive. Also, by not including a keyboard, the unit is compact and conserves on space. A synthesizer module in any shape or form is still an instrument because it produces music (even though it is not actually physically played).

Expanders, like synthesizers, may be supplied with a variety of pre-programmed sounds. Additional sounds may be loaded using 'RAM' or 'ROM packs' (data stored on chips), or via a cassette interface or disc. In this way, manufacturers provide access to a large assortment of sounds.

Samplers

The sampler is a digital recording device; it makes a digital map, or 'sample', of the waveform of a sound, and that sample, when played back, retains the characteristics of the original sound. Slices of sound are digitally recorded via microphone or direct line input into the sampler. Once inside the sample as a string of digits, the recorded sounds can be manipulated in a variety of ways (looped, reversed, filtered and so on), and then played back over the full range of the keyboard. The length of sample it is possible to record, and the quality of the recording, are dependent on the memory capacity of the sampler. The most powerful samplers can record several minutes' worth of sound at 44.1kHz (CD quality). Samplers come in a variety of forms: as keyboard devices, as modules, as software/ hardware add-ons to computers, and as dedicated sampling drum machines.

Drum machines 'Drum machines' are electronic devices that create drum sounds and can be used to replace the drummer in recording. With one of these units, you have an instant drummer at your disposal! Yes, automation is taking its toll in the music business, but at the same time, modern technology can be used to your benefit. As stated earlier in this chapter, there are pre-programmed, programmable and sampling drum machines.

Pre-programmed drum machines have a variety of internally stored rhythms that you can play by the touch of a button. These may include rock, country, disco, funky, blues, boogie, ballad, march, tango, cha-cha, bossa nova, samba, beguine, swing, waltz and polka. You can control the tempo, but you can't programme new patterns. If you're looking for a drum machine that is easy to operate and allows you to write over the rhythms set by the manufacturer (which are of standard musical genres), then this machine can help you. It is also the least expensive of all the drum machines.

With a programmable drum machine, you can make your own rhythmic patterns and set the combinations of drum sounds you want. You can select the time signature (such as $^4/_4$ or $^3/_4$) and the tempo (measured in beats per minute, or BPM). Among the sampled sounds from which you can select are the following: bass drum, snare drum, hi tom, medium tom, low tom, low conga, high conga, rim shot, crash cymbal, ride cymbal, shaker, timbale, closed hi-hat, open hi-hat, hand clap, low cowbell and hi cowbell.

Programmable drum machines have a variety of features that can help you in creating demos. Among these are 'quantisation', or 'auto-correction,' which corrects timing errors made when programming rhythmic patterns, and 'song mode,' which enables you to chain together the separate rhythmic patterns you may have for your verses. bridges or other sections of your songs.

Sampling drum machines are similar to programmable drum machines, except that they can play 'sampled' sounds of your choosing. If the sound you're sampling is electronic, you can play the instrument directly into the sampling drum machine. If it is an acoustic sound, you'll need a microphone. You plug the microphone directly into the sampling drum machine. This unit would be of interest to writers looking to create specific sounds in their recordings.

Electronic drum sets

There are also electronic drum sets that may not be of particular interest to songwriters unless they are drummers, but since they are another kind of modern electronic musical instrument, they will be briefly discussed. An electronic drum set is a group of pads connected to a 'brain' (a sound module), and set up like an acoustic drum kit. Sitting on a stool or chair, the drummer plays the pads with sticks, and triggers sounds stored in the 'brain' which can be heard through speakers. Each pad represents a different sound, and the sounds of a complete acoustic drum set can be recreated. Alternatively, you can get electronic drum sounds with the 'feel' of a live drummer.

CHAPTER FIVE

MIDI (MUSICAL INSTRUMENT DIGITAL INTERFACE)

MIDI (Musical Instrument Digital Interface) is a method of communicating performance data between various electronic musical instruments. Performance data refers to what notes are played and how they are played. The instruments are connected via MIDI cables to form a system where a single master controller (whether a keyboard, guitar, or sequencer) can control various external devices via MIDI. By using a sequencer to record MIDI data, multiple parts can be recorded and played back on various instruments, much the same as in using a multitrack tape recorder.

MIDI's distinct advantage over multitrack tape recording, however, is that it actually records the performances of an instrument (for example, the physical striking of piano keys) as opposed to the actual sounds of that keyboard. Thus when MIDI data is played back, you can choose new sounds or even send that performance to an entirely different instrument with its own sound producing characteristics. The MIDI specification is adhered to by all manufacturers in the electronic musical instrument industry. The specification is administered by the MIDI Manufacturers Association, a group of companies dedicated to maintaining the integrity of the interface.

There are two basic components in the MIDI system: the instrument or device transmitting the data, which is referred to as a controller, host, or master; and the instrument or device receiving and 'reading' the data, which is called the slave. Information is transmitted and received through special cables that connect to the units by a series of inputs and outputs called MIDI 'In' MIDI 'Out,' and MIDI 'Thru.' The most common MIDI instruments and devices include synthesizers, drum machines, sequencers, digital signal processing equipment (outboard gear), and master keyboard controllers.

MIDI as a tool for songwriting

MIDI is relatively new, having emerged in the early 1980s. Its future development and applications are hard to predict, as with any rapidly advancing technology. It has already been heralded as a milestone of the music business and of significant value for 'live' performers, musicians, producers, arrangers, composers and recording artists.

Essentially, MIDI enables one person (one set of hands) to play several instruments and sound-producing devices simultaneously. The applications of this phenomenon are astounding. With MIDI, there is no need to hire string players, woodwind players, percussionists, brass players and others. With MIDI, one person can be a duet or a combo, a stage band or a symphony orchestra. MIDI may be used to simulate a large ensemble performance both in the studio and in live performances such as in a concert hall.

MIDI permits songwriters to hear their music orchestrated— immediately. It allows them to use different sounds and rhythms to arrange their music. It enables songwriters to create and experiment with many different textures and to choose which ones complement others and which ones don't. Complex textures could be created that otherwise might not be achieved. The musically untrained songwriter will suddenly become aware of voicings. Perhaps most important of all, MIDI motivates. You'd only have to sit down at a master controller MIDI'd up to five or six other devices (additional units would be just that much more wonderful) to hear and be motivated by the powerful, dynamic and colourful sounds you can generate by each press of the keys. It's difficult to put into words that particular feeling you get when you have a world of music at your fingertips. Suffice to say, MIDI contains buried treasure just waiting to be unearthed by the songwriter.

There are various ways of experimenting or improvising to actually write a song. You may decide to 'jam' along with the sounds of a drum machine to create a song. The rhythm you choose will dictate a feel or 'groove' and may inspire you.

You might create a melodic bass line that could become the basis for a 'groove.' Or you could develop a pattern of chords around which you work a melody. Any approach could be used—it's an individual thing. Whatever the writer feels comfortable with is fine. You should continue to challenge yourself to be creative and try new approaches.

It should be noted that voices and acoustic instruments, such as horns, clarinets and violins, cannot be recorded via MIDI; only MIDI-controlled instruments can be recorded. But with a microphone, acoustic sounds may be digitally recorded into a sampler (see Chapter 4), and then those sounds can be controlled by MIDI.

How MIDI works

As we have already seen, a MIDI system consists of a controlling device and one or more slaves. In order to work, all the devices have to be connected together properly. This is done with cables that are plugged into the MIDI In, MIDI Out, and MIDI Thru jacks with which MIDI instruments are equipped. (Not all MIDI devices are equipped with a Thru jack, however.) These jacks are responsible for the three separate MIDI signal routes-in, out and thru. The sockets for these connections (which are all 5-pin DIN) are located on the rear panel of MIDI devices.

There is a single MIDI connection for each direction of signal flow between each instrument or device. The cable transmits high speed binary information in a 'serial' fashion; that is, the digital data is fed one piece at a time. This happens at such a high speed that the information can go to all the interconnected units and the sound from each will play virtually at once.

Most professional or hi-tech keyboards and expanders do not have built-in amplifiers. Some kind of an external amplifier is needed. In the case of MIDI keyboards, an audio mixer is also needed, for it provides the means to control the individual sound output levels of each of the MIDI devices. Thus the volume of string sounds can be controlled independently of that of the brass sounds. The mixer, in turn, must be connected to an amplification system (with speakers) so that the sounds may be heard (unlike many consumer keyboards which have built-in speakers).

How does a MIDI keyboard controller, for example, activate a digital drum machine? The keyboard can be used to play the sounds stored in the drum machine, with keyboard notes assigned to trigger drum machine sounds. (Usually it is the lowest octave of a keyboard that controls the drum machine sounds. A low C on the keyboard, for example, could be assigned to trigger the bass drum sound, the low D the snare drum sound, the low E the cymbal sound, and so forth.) Thus in laying down a track, a person could produce all the drum sounds with the keyboard controller connected to the drum machine. It may be more comfortable for some keyboard players to produce drum sounds with the large keys on the keyboard than with the smaller buttons of the drum machine.

There is another advantage of controlling the drum machine from a keyboard. Many drum machines are not fully dynamic. In other words, if you play a hi-hat sound, for instance, directly from the drum machine, you might only be able to get one or two different volume levels (depending on the machine) however hard you hit the pad, and this would lack the dynamic feel that acoustic drums can create. With a velocity sensitive keyboard, however, you can play the keyboard dynamically and transmit the dynamic information via MIDI to the drum machine. Therefore, if the key on the keyboard that triggers the snare drum is played softly, there will be a soft snare drum sound; if it is played hard, there will be a loud snare drum sound.

There are actually two functions of MIDI: 'live' performance and playback of a recorded performance. In the 'live' performance mode, a person playing a controller triggers all the other sound modules to play together simultaneously. In the playback of a recorded performance, the MIDI sequencer is used (see below). When the sequencer is activated, it sends previously 'recorded' performance data to the slaves, triggering the sounds of all the slaves at the same time. A 'live' player is only needed to turn on the sequencer 'play' switch!

Sequencers   The sequencer is a device that records, edits and plays back MIDI data. It does not 'record' actual sounds but stores digital data of performance 'events'—what notes are played, how hard or soft, pitch-bend, modulation and all other data related to the performance. Sequencers come in two primary forms: as self-contained, dedicated units, and as computer software. Software-based sequencers have the advantages of on-screen editing and convenient storage (on disc—a facility not all hardware sequencers have). Hardware sequencers have the benefit of portability, and are often preferred by 'gigging' musicians. Some keyboard synthesizers and samplers include an integrated sequencer,as, indeed, do drum machines.

The sequencer is a controller of information, and is not really a musical instrument. It is a multitrack MIDI event recorder, analogous to a multitrack tape recorder, and information can be overdubbed on it. A MIDI sequencer can record separate performances on each separate MIDI channel, much like recording on the separate tracks of a tape recorder. It is the modern-day equivalent of a player-piano mechanism, but uses a digital code instead of a perforated paper roll.

In the playback mode, the sequencer sends control information to the interconnected MIDI units, which are triggered and consequently play the stored data. A person is not needed at this point to do any actual playing.

In order to reproduce sonically the information stored in the sequencer, the MIDI Out of the sequencer must be fed into the various keyboards and expanders. The sound is reproduced 'first generation' (as opposed to using tapes, which suffer from signal deterioration). Remember, with a sequencer, no audio signals are stored—rather, the digital data corresponding to a performance is stored.

Like drum machines, sequencers have an internal 'clock,' a device that determines the tempo of a sequence. Consequently, a drum machine may be synchronized to a sequencer. The sequencer would be assigned as the master, and its clock set to control the clock rate of the drum machine.

The internal memory capacity of sequencers (particularly hardware sequencers) is limited. Consequently, instead of using up a sequencer's memory when MIDI'd to a drum machine, the latter may be programmed to use its own memory. Performance functions, such as pitch bend, can use up sequencer memory rapidly.

Sequencers can be programmed to have the sound modules connected to them to make sound changes during the course of a song. Thus a particular keyboard may have one sound for the verses and another for the choruses.

Prior to MIDI and sequencers, there was no way for one person to effect a complicated recording network without the use of a multitrack tape recorder. With the sequencer, experimentation can be done immediately, and textures can be altered effortlessly, even after they are captured or 'recorded,' until they are fine-tuned. Then when the information has been satisfactorily constructed and refined, it can be transferred and recorded onto tape. Thus MIDI sequencers are great money-saving devices because experimentation can be done at home—that is, the tracks can be worked out there—rather than in a commercial recording studio. Once all the tracks have been recorded into the MIDI sequencer, the sequencer, keyboards, expanders, and drum machine could be taken directly to a recording studio, where the sequenced tracks, including overdubs, may be transferred to multitrack tape.

In order to synchronize music on tape with a MIDI performance emanating from your sequencer, a sync tone must first be laid down on tape, allowing the tape to act as the master clock for the sequencer and thus allowing both devices to run at the same tempo. A sync tone is a series of audio pulses that can be used to drive the clock of an external sequencer. In order to record MIDI data with your sequencer while listening to music previously recorded on tape, this synchronization is necessary.

To make a tape copy at home, you would simply take the output of the mixer being used and feed it into the input of a cassette recorder or 2-track reel-to-reel tape recorder. Thus the MIDI path of information starts at the sequencer and goes to the keyboards and expanders, where the MIDI data is turned into audio signals, which are passed to the mixer; the audio signals from the mixer are then fed into the tape recorder.

A sequencer has the unique capability of time compression and time expansion. With time compression, you can have the sequencer speed up the tempo of a given passage or entire musical section without changing the pitch of the sound. Time expansion is the opposite. The sequencer can slow down the tempo without affecting the pitch. This is an advantage over tape, in which the pitch is changed when the multitrack machine is run faster or slower.

Benefits of the sequencer for songwriting

The sequencer may be looked upon as a tool for the craft of songwriting. It provides benefits even a multitrack tape recorder cannot offer.

The sequencer enables you to lay down parts on the keyboard and hear them back right away—no waiting for tape reels to rewind. The sequencer has a loop (continuous repeat) function, meaning that it can continuously play a particular section of music, enabling the songwriter to elaborate on and experiment with an idea while the loop is going. Thus with a MIDI sequencer, you do not have to constantly rewind tape to hear an idea continuously played back. You can overdub on a second keyboard or play live (work out new parts) without recording, until you create something with which you are satisfied (such as a harmony, groove or solo). It is an excellent vehicle with which to experiment and explore new melodies and sound textures.

Because of the error-correcting (quantization) feature that sequencers offer, slight timing irregularities during 'real-time' recording can be corrected, and the part will play as if executed perfectly and at whatever tempo is desired. MIDI sequencers also have a feature for 'non-player' musicians called 'step time.' With this, a person can enter in one note (or chord) at a time, the quantization-setting determining the rhythmic value of each note.

Sequencer editing functions

Sequencers have editing capability, that is, they are able to fix or change recorded passages. Although all sequencers have their own personalities, most include editing features such as the following:

1. *Copy*. A recorded passage or particular section can be repeated elsewhere in a composition by 'copying' that information to the new location.

2. *Insert*. Any number of blank measures can be inserted into a musical piece to expand the structure for later recording. For instance, if you have a song consisting of verses and choruses and want a bridge, you put in blank measures (consisting of rests) of the length of the bridge you want at that place in the song and then record the new part at that location.

3. *Delete*. Any specific bar or bars in a composition can be removed.

4. *Erase*. Everything after a particular point in a composition can be eliminated.

5. *Blank*. The contents of one or more bars can be removed, leaving the empty bar(s) in place. This enables a person to re-record a part correctly. In short, blanking allows mistakes to be removed and to be fixed by recording new parts.

It should be noted that information on any particular MIDI channel may be accessed and edited separately.

Most sequencers have back-up storage capability for all the data being recorded, either in the form of an audio cassette or of a computer disk. Both allow the user to store the MIDI information and identify it for later recall. This serves as a form of protection or back-up in the event that the data in 'working RAM' memory is accidentally lost while recording or editing.

MIDI interfacing

As previously mentioned, MIDI devices have three 5-pin DIN sockets into which special cables are plugged. The jacks are In, Out, and Thru. The principle of the interfacing is simple. MIDI In accepts incoming information, MIDI Out sends data out from the instrument, and MIDI Thru takes information received at MIDI In and passes it through the instrument to other instruments in the chain.

A basic set-up is as follows: the Out jack of the master keyboard is used to send data to the In of the next link (a keyboard or expander); the Thru jack of that unit is patched to the In jack of the next unit. So with MIDI, the original information from the host keyboard can not only control a single, linked unit, but can also pass through it and control the next unit, and so on in the series. Each subsequent unit receives information via its In jack and passes the data through (thru) to the next link.

When a sequencer is included in the set-up, the MIDI configuration becomes a little more involved. A typical MIDI patch using a sequencer is as follows: the MIDI Out of the master keyboard is patched to the sequencer's MIDI In. The sequencer's MIDI Out is then patched to the keyboard's MIDI In. This creates a circle, so that when you are recording, the sequencer will recognize performance information from the keyboard, and during playback, the keyboard will recognize performance information from the sequencer. The master keyboard's MIDI Thru is patched to the MIDI In of another keyboard or expander, and the MIDI Thru of that unit would be patched to another keyboard or expander, and so on, depending upon the number of units linked in the MIDI chain. The last device in any MIDI chain has no cable connected to its MIDI Out or to its MIDI Thru—just the MIDI In is used.

Remember, if one keyboard and one expander were to be interfaced, only a single cable would be needed. The cable would go from the MIDI Out of the host keyboard to the MIDI In of the expander. If another expander were to be used, then the MIDI Thru of the first expander would be patched into the MIDI In of the second expander, and so forth.

If all this sounds confusing, that's because it is. The real learning of MIDI comes with actually setting up the system. Start simply and then increase in complexity. As you create more complicated networks, you'll also find the sounds you are producing are more exciting, too. Once you get the hang of it, you'll find MIDI an important tool for writing and making demos.

Fig. 6 BASIC MIDI/AUDIO CONNECTIONS

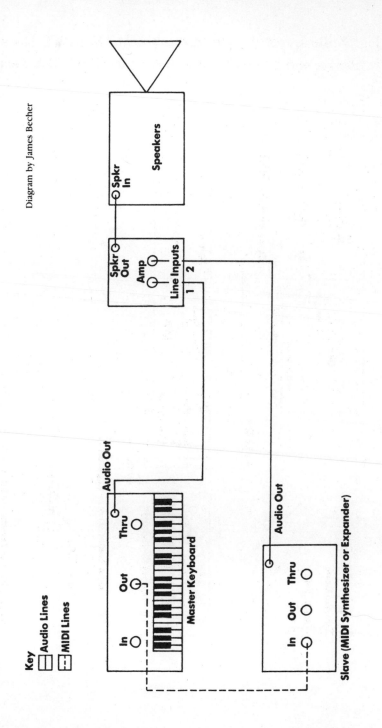

Diagram by James Becher

Key
- Audio Lines
- MIDI Lines

Speakers

Spkr In

Spkr Out

Amp

Line Inputs

1   2

Audio Out

Thru   Out   In

Master Keyboard

Audio Out

In   Out   Thru

Slave (MIDI Synthesizer or Expander)

Fig. 6 illustrates the most basic use of MIDI.

Fig. 7 illustrates a more elaborate MIDI patch, showing how a sequencer and drum machine may be used in a MIDI set-up.

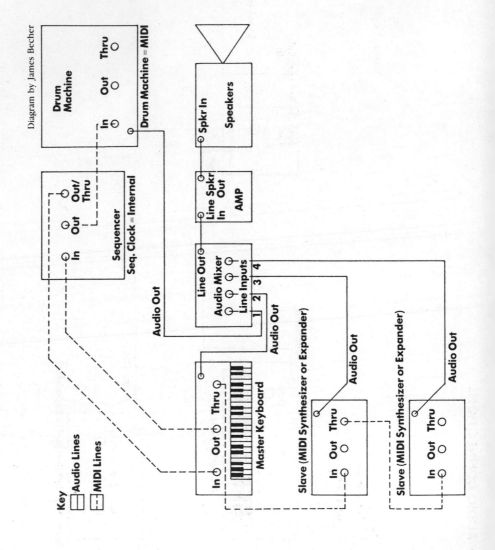

Fig. 7 MORE COMPLEX MIDI/AUDIO CONNECTIONS

Diagram by James Becher

Note: Some sequencers have two MIDI Outs and a 'mix' function which allows the signal at the MIDI Out to be a mix of the incoming MIDI In signal as well as the sequencer data.

MIDI master keyboard controller

The instrument generating the original performance data in a MIDI set-up is referred to as the master. This could be the sequencer (as previously described), but is often a keyboard synthesizer. There is, however, another type of keyboard that looks like a conventional synthesizer (it has a full keyboard) but is not a conventional synthesizer because no sound emanates from it. This is the MIDI master keyboard controller, often known just as a 'master' or 'mother' keyboard. It is dedicated to providing versatile control information to the MIDI expanders and devices. Since the MIDI master keyboard does not have to generate any sound, all its microprocessor power is devoted to control information. This includes the ability to split a keyboard into playing zones.

A master keyboard, for example, may have two split-points, creating three playing zones. Each of the zones can be assigned its own MIDI channel, which expanders and other keyboards would be set up to receive on. For example, the left zone may be assigned to one synthesizer, the middle zone to an expander, and the right zone to another synthesizer. The zones could even be set up to overlap. The two synthesizers could be assigned to cover the entire keyboard, with adjacent but non-overlapping zones, while the expander could be assigned to the middle section of the keyboard only, overlapping the top end of the left zone (i.e. the lowest part of the master keyboard) and the bottom end of the right zone. The left zone of the keyboard would sound one synthesizer and the right zone another synthesizer. However, since the zones overlap, the middle zone would control not only the expander assigned to it but also both of the other synthesizers. (By creating the split points, you are actually selecting the range of the keyboard that you want these devices to play.)

Let's examine a hypothetical situation. By creating split points, you could assign the left zone of the master keyboard, to play a bass sound of an expander (on its own separate MIDI channel), the middle zone to play an organ, and the right zone to play an effect, such as a splash, explosion or bell chime. It would be as if you're playing three different keyboards. Better still, the master keyboard can be used to call up specific sounds on the external devices. You're eliminating the need to have to change sounds from the three keyboards individually: the change can be effected by the push of a single button on the master keyboard.

Home MIDI studio

As equipment and instruments become less expensive and songwriters more concerned about the quality of their demos, the home MIDI studio is becoming more common. Basically, it consists of synthesizers, expanders, a drum machine and a sequencer. The sequencer functions as the 'control centre.' A master keyboard is not typically found in the home studio.

The MIDI studio serves two basic purposes. It lets songwriters work out ideas for compositions, and it may be used for pre-production. With MIDI instruments you can create almost all the parts of an arrangement—the bass part, several keyboard lines, the drum part, solo instrumental parts and so forth. These parts may be stored in the sequencer (as digital information or performance data) and played back. You can sit back and listen to it, and if you're not happy with the entire sound or any part of it, you can change and edit the arrangement. Finally, after all the parts have been programmed to your satisfaction and stored into the internal memory of the sequencer, you can copy the contents of the internal memory to a cassette or floppy disk for back-up storage.

The advantage of the MIDI studio with respect to pre-production is that having worked out most of the arrangement of your song at home, you can go into any studio you want—even an expensive digital studio—and lay down your tracks onto tape in a matter of hours. You merely set up your instruments and equipment (including, of course, the sequencer) in the studio, plug into the mixing console, get levels, and *voilà!*—all the instruments play as you programmed them! You save a great deal of money by having worked out the parts at home rather than in the studio, and also by not having to pay other musicians to record in the studio.

The prices of equipment and instruments are coming down, and a rudimentary home MIDI studio consisting of synthesizer, sequencer, drum machine, 4-track 'portastudio' (a combined mixer/ multitrack recorder), amplifier and monitor speakers, can be set up for as little as £2,000 or less. But add some signal processing, a couple of synthesizer modules, a sampler and better-quality recording equipment, and things can start getting quite a bit more expensive. The prices of some synthesizers and other equipment of quality can range from one thousand to more than fifteen thousand pounds. However, when you add up all the money saved from studio rentals and musicians' fees, you might find that the system will eventually pay for itself. And you get the benefits of being able to record whenever you want in the comfort of your home.

CHAPTER SIX

COMPUTERS AND COMPUTER SOFTWARE

Computers, those extraordinary machines that perform incredible functions for mathematicians, astronomers, corporations, law enforcement agencies, bankers and just about everyone else, are also a boon for songwriters. Years ago, it might have been hard to imagine a machine like this assisting in the musical creative process, but it has indeed become a major asset to the songwriter's and musician's trade. Computers and their software are now regular fixtures in recording studios, commercial and home alike.

Essentially, computers may be used as a medium for storing, remembering and retrieving data which may be heard as music when connected with appropriate synthesizers. Magnetic tape, of course, is a medium for recording and playing back sound, but there are advantages in using computers, including speed and compactness of the software. Specific songs or individual parts of songs can be retrieved faster with the computer than with tape. Computer disks are also less bulky than recording tape.

MIDI is the means to store and retrieve performances on computer. To make tape copies to submit as demos, you link up a system in which MIDI (not audio) signals travel from the computer to the instruments which recreate your original keyboard parts. The audio output from the instruments travels to the mixing board and to a multitrack tape recorder, and to speakers so you can hear the sounds. You mix the multitrack tape down to a two-track stereo recording that could be used to make tape copies for submission to publishers, labels, record producers, artists and ad agencies (or jingle houses). Computers may be used then to make demos at home. If you have only a 4- or 8-track tape recorder at home, you can take your software to a professional studio with a 24-track machine, for example, unload the musical information on the computer to the 24-track tape using the synth arsenal of the studio, and have many open tracks to continue working on your recording. The basic tracks can be worked out at home and overdubbed at the studio. Indeed, a master quality recording could be obtained in this way. By doing the basic tracks at home, you'd be saving a lot of money. To retrieve the data (keyboard parts) from the computer in the studio, however, your computer must be compatible with the one in the studio. You would also need similar instruments at the studio for the computer to transmit signals through.

Functions and benefits

Computers may be used to make demos, but they also may serve more specific functions, depending on the particular software used. Functions are performed by interfacing—although not necessarily through MIDI—the computer with musical instruments. There are many different programs that are designed for varied uses. Computers and computer software may be used by songwriters to:

- view and change the sound/parameters and settings of most synthesizers
- work out ideas and create complex arrangements
- store sound samples (in the form of digital data)
- notate music
- learn about music

The benefits of computers and their software, then, are that they can be used to manipulate and organize musical ideas and arrangements into a logical format, build a library of sounds, and make graphic representations of digitally stored musical information for editing. If you cannot read or write music, the musical notation program will provide you with the equivalent of a manuscript or lead sheet of your music. There is educational value in software that teaches music theory, harmony, orchestration, ear training, sight singing, keyboard playing and other subjects. Ultimately, the computer may be deemed a tool of inspiration. By using the computer to aid in the creation and alteration of sounds, ideas can be born. Textures of sound may be created that will steer the creative process in specific directions.

Software

The computer may be looked at as a data organization and storage device. It takes information and organizes it into user-definable filing systems. Software programmes are the actual means by which information is manipulated and managed. Music software falls into four basic categories.

1. MIDI sequencing software
2. patch librarian/editing software
3. music printing software
4. music education software

MIDI sequencing software

Sequencing software programmes record and store performances on any MIDI instrument and let you change, edit, expand, condense and correct musical information once you have put it in the computer. You can move sections of the song around, change the parameters of any note in the song, and increase or decrease the tempo, etc.

Patch librarian/editing software

Patch librarian and patch editing software are also used to store information, but instead of musical performance data they give a full screen display of the parameters of sounds created on a synthesizer. Graphic representations of sound make it easier for you to create new sounds. You can generate waveforms, edit harmonic content and other parameters of sound on the screen, and alter the 'knob' settings in the synthesizer (which results in changes in the sound you hear). In summary, you can create and organize libraries of sounds using this software. Programmes are also available for sample-editing.

Music printing software

Music printing software enables you to print on paper the musical information that you put into the computer from a keyboard or other MIDI instrument. This may include not only a melody line but also bass parts and overdubs—up to a full orchestral score. It displays the data on the screen, and you can type in lyrics, chord symbols and other information before you print it out. Music printing software also lets you transpose or extract individual parts. This software is particularly beneficial for songwriters who can't notate music.

Music Education Software

Music education software may be of interest to songwriters looking to improve their musical skills or educate themselves in areas where they lack training. There are programmes covering various subjects, including ear training and harmony.

CHAPTER SEVEN

HOME RECORDING

For many years, quality recording was the domain of commercial recording studios. In recent years, however, the home has emerged as both a hi-tech workshop for working out ideas on tape or computer, and an environment for making professional-sounding demos and even masters. There are many reasons for this: the technological revolution, the availability of semi-pro equipment at affordable prices, the convenience of working at home, the desire to have control over the equipment and the recording and mixing processes, discouragement with the high prices of commercial studios, and the fact that once the initial investment for the equipment has been made, you're basically your own studio— advance bookings do not have to be made, a musician can record at any time of day or night, and 'studio' time is free. The only costs are for tape and electricity.

In Chapter Three, we discussed the professional recording studio. Depending on your recording system at home, the difference between your set-up and a commercial studio's may be just a matter of scale—how many tracks are available, what outboard equipment there is, and to an extent, quality—equipment and acoustics at home are not on par with the studios. For demos though, you don't need a state-of-the-art studio, just a home system that will yield quality recordings.

As a matter of fact, by being able to spend an unlimited number of hours perfecting a demo at home on a 4-track tape recorder, for instance, you might be able to get an even better product than if you recorded for a limited time in a commercial studio on an 8- or 16- track machine. You may experiment, rework ideas, and record over and over again at home, whereas in a commercial studio, your budget may prevent you from making the demo you really want.

If you take the time and effort to learn about home studio equipment and its operation, you'll be serving your career well. In today's musical arena, where the 'sound' of a record is almost as important as the song itself, knowing the kinds and capabilities of instruments and equipment available will help you tremendously. It is sometimes difficult to convey to an engineer exactly what type of sound or groove you want. When you understand electronic equipment, you can manipulate it yourself and your world of creating sounds will be greatly enhanced. Of course, not everybody can be an engineer, but basic skills can be learned by anyone who takes the time.

Electronic recording

In Chapter Two, 'Multitrack Recording and Mixing,' we discussed multitrack recording. Using certain instruments and equipment at home, you can record all the tracks yourself, as opposed to a 'live' session where a group of musicians come into a studio and lay down tracks together.

You can record using a multitrack tape recorder, a sequencer or a computer with sequencer software. If you use a multitrack tape recorder (such as a 4-track cassette), you can record many parts by using the technique of bouncing, also covered in Chapter Two. If you use a sequencer, you will similarly lay down parts one at a time, but instead of being recorded onto tape, they will go into the sequencer's memory. After all the parts have been recorded into the sequencer, you can transfer them to tape so you can make copies for yourself. To do this, you'll be connecting your sequencer, instruments, mixer and tape recorder together.

In Chapter Six, 'Computers and Computer Software,' we covered how computers are used to make demos. You can make demos at home, or take your software into a studio and do your overdubs onto a 16- or 24-track recorder. If your software isn't compatible with the studio's computer, you can bring your own computer to the studio.

What do you need to begin a home studio? To start, you'll need an electronic instrument, a microphone, a tape recorder and a monitor system. The electronic instrument you'll have greatest flexibility with is a keyboard, but it doesn't necessarily have to be that. If you play electric guitar, it will do just fine. As for the tape recorder, it can be a 4-track cassette deck or a multitrack reel-to-reel tape recorder (4-, 8- or 16-track recorders are what home recordists use). The 4-track cassette recorder is extremely popular with songwriters today. More about that later.

Other instruments and equipment may be added as you can afford them. You'll need a mixer to control the signal you're recording. Fortunately, most portable multitrack cassette recorders have mixers already built in. If you have a reel-to-reel deck, you'll need a separate mixer, though. You might also want to add a drum machine, a sequencer, a computer and signal processors.

The following list summarizes the minimum and optional instruments and equipment that the songwriter should have for a home studio.

Needed
- electronic or electric instrument (keyboard, guitar, bass)
- microphone
- multitrack tape recorder
- mixer
- mixdown tape recorder
- power amplifier
- monitors (speakers)
- headphones
- appropriate cables

Optional

- synthesizer(s)
- guitar
- drum machine
- expander(s)
- sequencer
- computer and software
- digital delay unit
- reverberation unit
- compressor/limiter
- noise gate/expander

It should be noted that owning a mixdown tape recorder is not actually necessary. If you do not own one and know someone who does, you can mix down your multitrack tape to a 2-track stereo recording by plugging into that person's machine. Or you can use a stereo cassette tape recorder. You may also mix down in a commercial studio, although you'll have to pay for time.

As you can see, by recording at home, you can make your demos yourself. You don't need 'live' musicians, who traditionally were required for recording. You're your own band! If you record at home, you're more likely to have all your electronic instruments and equipment close to your recorder so that you can play your instruments and operate the equipment from one chair. Now that's progress—engineering and performing out of the same seat!

4-track cassette tape recorders

As mentioned earlier in this chapter, 4-track cassette tape recorders are very popular with songwriters today. You might consider this as the system to start with. These units currently have up to eight input channels, and with bouncing, you can record ten or more parts—or more still if you can record several parts simultaneously (for instance by using a sequencer). The units have monitor outputs and noise reduction systems.

Fig. 8 RECORDING AND BOUNCING TRACKS ON A 4-TRACK CASSETTE RECORDER

TRK 1	A(1,2,3,4)		E(1,2,3,4)		H(1,2,3,4)		J(1,2,3,4) 4
TRK 2	B(1,2,3,4)	F(1,2,3,4)				H,J(4+3)	H,J(4+3) 7
TRK 3	C(1,2,3,4)		E,F,G (4+4+2)	E,F,G	E,F,G	E,F,G	E,F,G (4+4+2) 10
TRK 4		A,B,C,D (4+4+4+1)	A,B,C,D	A,B,C,D	A,B,C,D	A,B,C,D	A,B,C,D (4+4+4+1) 13

First, three tracks of the 4-track tape are recorded, with up to four parts on each track.

These tracks are then mixed for proper balance and rerecorded on the fourth track while simultaneously adding a new part via the mixer.

Up to four new parts are then recorded on each of tracks one and two.

Tracks one and two are then transferred to track three with the addition of up to two new parts.

Up to four new parts are then recorded on track one.

Track one is transferred to track two while adding up to three new parts via the mixer.

This leaves just one open track on which up to four more parts are recorded. The total number of possible parts recorded without going beyond the second generation is 34.

In recording with a cassette tape recorder, you lay down parts and continually bounce them over to open tracks. The technique of bouncing was discussed in Chapter Two. With your own multitrack recorder, you can overdub as you go along, and if you're not happy with a part, you can erase it (so long as you haven't bounced yet). You can come up with new lines or shape existing ones as you wish. This enables you to work out a song and the demo at the same time. Fig. 8, taken from *Are You Ready For Multitrack?* (TEAC Corporation), further illuminates the process of recording and bouncing on a 4-track tape recorder.

There is equipment that facilitates recording on your own. For example, a remote punch in/punch out foot switch will enable you to operate the recorder from several feet away. While your hands are on your instrument, you can use your foot to activate the tape machine and record a new performance over a pre-existing one to get a better track, or to 'punch in' a section of music if you played a mistake.

After you have recorded on all four tracks, you'll need to mix them down to get a 2-track master. As mentioned before, you can mix down to a regular consumer-model stereo cassette tape recorder.

'Live' recording Recording at home doesn't have to be by the electronic methods just described. You can set up a studio, much like a professional studio, where 'live' musicians and singers can record. Everything will just be on a smaller scale, but you'll get quality recordings.

Microphones

Different types of microphones are used in various situations. The type used may depend upon whether it is for recording or for live performance, pop or classical music, a loud or soft instrument. There are basically two types of microphone, in terms of construction and converting sound (acoustic) energy into electrical energy: 'dynamic,' which work on *electromagnetic* principles, and 'condenser,' which work on electrostatic principles.

There are two varieties of dynamic microphones. One is the 'moving coil' microphone, in which a coil moves through a fixed magnetic field and creates an electrical signal. The other is the 'ribbon' microphone, in which a fine sheet of metal foil moves through a fixed magnetic field and creates an electrical signal. Each of these microphones responds to variations in air pressure.

Dynamic microphones, particularly the moving coil variety, are used for extremely high sound-pressure levels such as an electric guitar playing rock, or where the microphone might be subjected to rough treatment, such as in a live concert.

Ribbon microphones are generally used where a coloration or warmth from the low frequency spectrum is desired. They would probably be used for singing and acoustic instruments.

'Condenser' microphones are generally all-purpose microphones. They have a wide bandwidth, which means they are capable of reproducing clearly the full frequency spectrum. They are known for their brilliance and accuracy.

Any of the above-mentioned microphones can be manufactured to have certain 'directional' characteristics. That is, the microphones can be made to discriminate in their sensitivity to acoustical energy relative to where the sound is coming from. In this respect, there are 'unidirectional' or 'figure of eight' microphones, 'cardioid,' 'omnidirectional,' and 'bidirectional'.

Acoustics

If you're going to record at home electronically, the instruments will plug directly into your hardware, so acoustics won't be of great concern. But if you record 'live,' you should attempt to make the recording environment as 'dead' (sound absorbent) as possible (as opposed to a 'live' room, such as a gymnasium, where sounds are reflected. A rule of thumb for home recordists is: the smaller the room, the 'deader' the room should be. A 'deadened' room will have sound-absorbent material on the walls and ceiling. This may be accomplished inexpensively with egg crate foam (obtained from commercial packing firms); batting (the material used for stuffing quilts, obtained from fabric stores); or egg cartons (these are not really sound absorbent because they are not very porous, but they do diffuse sound because of their shape, and hence take some of the 'boxiness' out of rooms). Alternatively, you may find that things like carpets, curtains, books and upholstered furniture already provide adequate, or nearly adequate acoustic damping in your room.

The thickness of sound-absorbent materials in a room may be made to vary in different sections. For instance, an area designated for recording vocals may be padded with double thickness material. Also, 'hard' furniture may be covered with blankets. With a 'deadened' room, you want to eliminate reflections as much as possible and focus solely on the sound emanating from the speakers.

Demos vs. masters

With a thin line often separating demos from masters, how exactly are they distinguished? Generally, demos and masters may be differentiated by the following:

Performance level. The performances on masters must be virtually perfect. Recordists will take the time and effort to achieve this level, punching in even single notes or syllables. MIDI, sequencers and computers make it easier to achieve performance perfection, and you can use these machines to bring the level of performance on your demo up to professional standards.

Extent of recording. With masters, many, many parts will be laid down until the producer is satisfied that the recording has everything it needs. With demos, you don't have to overdub to that extent.

Care. Greater care will go into making a master. More time will be spent adding special effects to get the sound you want. In both recording and mixing, the engineer will try to maximize the performances.

Equipment. Although some artists today record at home, most masters are still made in commercial studios. Home equipment is of good quality, but not of the calibre of professional recording equipment. You can make good recordings on home gear, but professional equipment can do it better.

At home you can spend more time trying to perfect your demos, and this might bring them up to (or surpass) the quality of a recording you'd get in the studio, where the financial clock is ticking away.

With good engineering practices and sufficient experience with home equipment, you should be able to record a product that is acceptable on a professional level.

As a final word on the technical aspects of making demos, it should be said that while books are useful, the only real way to learn is by actually *doing* it. Indeed, there's a lot of 'hands-on' experience you'll need—operating a multitrack tape recorder, bouncing, mixing, recording with synthesizers, programming drum machines, using sequencers and computers. Many problems will arise, but you can solve these by asking questions and experimenting, that's how you'll become adept.

CHAPTER EIGHT

SUBMITTING YOUR DEMOS

When you have completed your demos to your satisfaction, you are ready to begin the submission process. This is a task many songwriters dread because it is a business (and non-creative) activity; they have to put up with lack of responses to their phone calls and letters; and, worst of all, they have to face inevitable rejection. The word 'inevitable' is used because every songwriter, amateur and professional alike, sees their material turned down. (Music history is rife, however, with stories of songs rejected by superstars that go on to become hits for others.) If you can accept rejection as an unavoidable and realistic part of being a songwriter, and believe in your music enough so that any rejection won't diminish your enthusiasm for it, then you have a professional attitude, and it is songwriters with professional attitudes who endure, sustain, and are most likely to succeed.

The future of your songs (not to mention your songwriting career!) depends on the outcome of the submission process, so needless to say, it is vital, and must be approached methodically and intelligently. At this point you have spent a great deal of time (and money) making your demos, and you're eager to 'capitalize' on your investment, not just for financial remuneration but also in an artistic sense, to see your songs come to life and be enjoyed by people everywhere.

The submission process may be boiled down to the following elements: study and awareness, casting your songs, making copies of your demo, registering your songs for copyright, preparing the demo package, sending out your demos, attending meetings, and devising new strategies. Each of these considerations is examined in this chapter. (Following up on mailings is discussed in Chapter Nine, 'Keeping Records.')

Study and awareness

To become a successful songwriter requires you to be an astute observer of the music industry. It's not enough just to write songs and hope for the best. You must be aware of people in music publishing and record companies, of what artists and producers are making the charts, and of who is looking for material. It is also beneficial to know who the heavy-hitting personal managers and lawyers are, when industry conventions are held (so that you may attend), and where songwriting organization workshops and meetings take place. In addition to all this, it helps to know as much about the music business as possible, including the latest developments in record company practices, audio technology, copyright law, union regulations, video and other areas. Indeed, the education you should be acquiring is an ongoing process. But it should also be fun, and you don't have to go to college for it. Your music business education will happen in a variety of places, including your home, your local library, and your car (if you drive and have a radio); you can also learn by talking to people who have valuable information to offer.

Reading the music press

The most important source of industry news is the music press. Among the principal publications are the weekly music papers—*Melody Maker, New Musical Express* and *Sounds*—the trade papers—*Music Week* and *Studio Week*—and the music technology magazines—*Sound On Sound, Music Technology, Home and Studio Recording*. Between them, these will give you the latest news, including who's been recently hired by companies, what artists have just been signed to record with what companies, what songwriters have been signed to publishing deals, what new companies are forming, what's going on at the rights organizations (PRS, MCPS, PPL and VPL), new developments in music technology, and much more. You should take advantage of the news you read. People beginning jobs in new companies, such as A& R men, might be particularly on the lookout for fresh talent.

One of the most important features of the music and trade papers is the charts. There are all sorts of charts: singles, albums, 'Indie' (for releases by the 'Independent' record labels), dance, country, and so on. These should be studied. As well as the names of artists and songwriters, the Music Week singles charts provide the names of producers, record labels and publishers. If one of your songs is in the same vein as a chart-maker, you now know *who* to reach, and it's just a matter of contacting them. Subscribing to all these publications would be expensive, but you should be able to find them at your local library. If you are intrigued about the system by which music is created and disseminated around the world, and curious about what is happening in the lives of other writers and musicians, then you should enjoy reading the music press. In addition, consumer-oriented entertainment magazines like *Q* and *The Face* might also have information that could help you. If you are ambitious and diligent enough, you should clip articles of interest and place them in a file. Cut the articles out, date them, and write on them the name of the publication they came from. By maintaining a file of 'contacts,' you may have a ready-made list of leads when you are ready to send out your songs.

Other sources of information

The *Music Week* annually publishes the Music Week Directory, which contains the names, addresses, and phone numbers of music publishers and record labels (among other companies). This is an extremely valuable source for finding where to reach many of the people to whom you'll want to submit demo tapes.

The radio will serve as a means of practical education for you. Tune into stations that play the type of music that you write or would like to write, but be sure these have a playlist rotation of the latest hits. It's not that you should imitate what's out, but you should be aware of what kind of songs are well received, what sounds are 'happening,' and other trends in contemporary music. You should also be on the lookout for artists who may be suitable to sing your songs.

Much information can be uncovered from a visit to a record shop. The backs of album jackets contain a wealth of information, and it might be to your advantage to jot some of those credits down. Look for people to submit your songs to for appropriate artists. The producer, A& R coordinator at the record label, personal manager and even the engineer are potential contacts. You might feel nervous about contacting them out of the blue, and you may not always get an encouraging response, but remember, your career is at stake.

Casting your songs

While you are studying the music industry, which as we said before is a continuous process, you will be writing new songs. You should be 'casting' your songs as you write them. Much as a motion picture casting director tries to find the actors most suited for a particular new film, you should try to determine those artists who might be candidates to record your songs. If you have a wonderful ballad, a singer who has had a hit or two singing ballads is someone you should contact. If your tune is funky and rhythmic, try artists who have been successful with such songs. But also be observant and innovative. Maybe that funky artist needs to be perceived by the public as a multi-talented singer, and needs a poignant and melodic ballad. You might also try reaching artists who haven't had a hit in several years. They might be looking for fresh, contemporary songs to bring them to the attention of record companies and the public again.

When casting your songs, don't consider singer-songwriters, that is, people who write their own material. These people rarely record other people's songs. It's not that they don't want to give anyone else a chance, but they prefer to maintain an image that includes 'writer of songs.'

Of course, if you send your material to music publishers, the A&R people there will cast your songs themselves, if they like them and want to sign them. But in your covering letter, you still might want to indicate those particular artists for whom you feel your songs are appropriate.

Your knowledge of artists, gained from listening to the radio, watching television, going to clubs, and reading the trades, will determine how you cast your songs. But you should also get feedback from other people. Play your songs for friends and family alike; they may come up with artists you didn't think of.

Making copies of your demo

Earlier in the book, it was stated that your multitrack demo master will be a mixed down 2-track stereo tape. If you record in mono, your original tape is your master. Whatever your master is, never submit it. You use it to make copies from and for nothing else. Keep it in a safe place and at about room temperature. Don't make copies from copies. The more generations you go, the worse the fidelity. Your master is the only tape you should make copies from. Treat it with respect!

There are various mediums in which to reproduce sound recordings: cassette tape, reel-to-reel tape and disk. Today, cassette tapes are most commonly used because of several advantages: they are easy to play, convenient to mail or carry, and have good audio fidelity (this has improved greatly since they were first introduced to the public in 1964).

Your tape and tape box should bear your name, address and telephone number, as well as the names of the songs and any other pertinent information (for example, tape speed if reel-to-reel tape is used, or whether the recording was made with noise reduction). There is not much room to write on cassette labels, but you should at least include your name, phone number and the names of the songs.

If you use cassettes, don't forget to take out those little squares on the rear spine. These prevent erasure that could happen accidentally or (heaven forbid!) intentionally.

How many songs should you include on your tape? As a general rule, no more than four; two or three is fine. The thing to bear in mind is that you should include your best songs only; those tunes that hopefully have commercial hit potential. Perhaps you might put on a song that wouldn't really be a hit but shows another dimension of your talent. Limit this to one song only. People in the music business are looking for hits; for album fillers they can go to their mothers or nephews. Repeat, use discretion. Don't think that because you've got a cassette tape, you have to fill it up or include half your catalogue. Include no more than three or four of your best, most commercial hit-oriented songs. Put the best song (in your opinion) up front, the second best song next, and so forth.

If you are using tape, record on one side only and make sure it is rewound to the beginning and ready to play. You'll make an immediate poor impression if you submit a cassette tape that has to be rewound to get to the first song.

You should space the songs on your demo tape so the listener will know when one song ends and a new one begins. Adding space on your tape will also give him a short break in between songs. But people don't like to wait too long either, so don't keep them waiting. In general, songs should be spaced anywhere from two to four seconds apart.

Registering your songs for copyright

After you decide to whom to send your material, the next step is to actually send it out. Of course, you might be worried about 'protecting' your songs, and if you haven't already, now is the time to do so.

There is no formal procedure for the registration of copyright in the UK (as there is in the USA), but a dated copy may be lodged with a bank or solicitor. Alternatively, you can send it to yourself by registered post, or, for a fee, you can enter your song on the private registry of Stationer's Hall (Ave Maria Lane, London EC2M 7DD) where they will keep a dated copy for seven years, after which period it becomes necessary to re-register the song. Any of these methods will provide proof of authorship in the case of a legal dispute.

Preparing the demo package

You went to great lengths (and perhaps expense) to make your demos. Don't undermine your efforts and talent by presenting a package that reflects an uncaring, sloppy or lazy person and which might turn off the listeners.

Although the bottom line in terms of acceptance or rejection of your song will be the listener's perception of its potential, you should make sure that your package shows you to be a true professional who *cares* about his or her work. There's a psychological factor involved. When a person receives a package that is put together sloppily, reads a letter with many misspelled words and grammar that looks like it was written by an elementary school dropout, he or she cannot help but have low expectations for the material. That could make some difference when the demo is listened to. To get a song accepted is an uphill battle anyway. You certainly don't want to enter the arena with a disadvantage before confrontation begins.

There are two ways to submit a demo: by post or by playing it in person. If you are sending it in the post, your package will consist of three items: a covering letter, the demo and a self-addressed stamped envelope. When posting your package, send it first class in an envelope large enough to accommodate all its contents neatly.

Covering letters

In your covering letter, make clear exactly what it is you are pursuing. Do you want your song to be considered for publishing? Do you want it considered for a particular artist? Do you want the performer on your demo to be considered for a record contract? If it is intended that the artist (you or someone else or a group) on the demo be considered for a deal, include also a bio and a black and white photograph.

Your covering letter should be brief and neat. It should have your name, address and telephone number. This is so elementary it seems almost ridiculous to say, but it is guaranteed that there are some songwriters who after all their work, absent-mindedly omit one or more of these elements. The letter should be typed, or neatly printed or written. A few paragraphs will suffice—don't go into a discourse about your life and your music. Of course, if you will be playing your demo at a personal meeting, you might want to prepare an information sheet, or anything that you feel would help or would enthuse the auditioner.

You will be sending letters to various markets—artists, producers, managers and others—and your covering letters should be tailored to each market. There are no set rules, other than those mentioned above concerning succinctness and neatness, and you will get a better feel for writing letters as you go along.

Here are a few sample covering letters:

Dear [Record Producer]*

Your recent success with 'Urge Me On' by Al Smith has prompted me to send two songs for your consideration: 'Come On Baby' and 'Let's Go Now.' I think you will find these fit with Mr. Smith's current style, but also have a groove that would move him further in a New Wave direction.

I am a 21-year-old songwriter who has been composing for eleven years. I perform with my group Churn at local clubs.

Thanks for your interest.

Yours sincerely,

*Insert name

Dear [Record Producer]

My group Gulp! has a large following in the London club scene. We're a soft rock band, doing mostly originals but some covers. We have also played at benefits and on local TV shows.

At this point in our career we are looking for a recording contract. This comes after years of evolving as a musical unit and developing our song writing.

Rather than approaching a record company directly, we want the opportunity of working with a producer we respect and feel would understand our music and be able to take us in the direction we want to pursue. Based on your experience with artists such as Cat Man Boy and The Yellow Wolves, we believe you could help us in our careers.

Enclosed for your consideration is a demo tape of three songs, 'Yell, Yell, Yell,' 'Have It Already,' and 'Girls Have It All,' as well as a bio and photograph of the group.

I would be most grateful if you could take time from your busy schedule and listen to our tape.

Yours sincerely,

Dear [Music Publisher]

I am a prolific writer of rock and rhythm & blues songs. I believe my material, which has catchy hooks, witty lyrics, and is up-to-date (forgive my modesty!), has enormous commercial potential. A wide range of artists would be suitable to record my songs.

Enclosed for your consideration is a demo containing four tunes. If these are of interest to you, I would be happy to send more or meet with you at your convenience.

Yours sincerely,

Dear [Artist's Manager]

I was wondering if you would be so kind as to pass along the enclosed demo tape to Sy James, or his producer, Bo Beans. I have been trying to reach either party but without success. I think the songs on the tape, which have tremendous hit potential, are perfect for the direction James is going in.

Of course, I hope that you will listen to the tape first, and I have no doubt that after hearing it, you will share my enthusiasm.

Thanks in advance.

Yours sincerely,

Sending out your demos

There are two things to say here: do it and don't be afraid to! Your songs have no chance of getting recorded and commercially released if they're not exposed to people who can make it happen. And the more tapes you have out, the better your chances for getting a deal.

Some songwriters have reservations about exposing a song for fear that it might be 'ripped off.' For these writers, however, it's a Catch-22 situation: if you show your music, it can get ripped off; if you don't, it will never get recorded.

To get recorded, a song not only has to be heard, but it must also usually be widely exposed. Chances are that it will not get placed on the first or second audition, but on the eighth or ninth or fifteenth. Just be sure it is submitted to reputable people, those who work for *bona fide* companies or have solid track records.

There's no limit to the number of markets to which you may send your demo. Your only limitations are those of making tape copies, typing covering letters, mailing the packages, and coming up with potential markets. If you feel your song must get to one particular artist, you can try his producer, record label, music publisher, personal manager or solicitor. You want to maximize your chances for getting the song to that artist.

Meetings

Every attempt should be made to have a meeting in which your demo could be played while you are present. There are a number of reasons for this: you'll *know* your tape was actually listened to; you get to meet a valuable contact who will now remember you and probably keep an open door for you and your songs; you'll get instant feedback (reasons why your material is good or deficient in some way); you may get advice on how to improve your writing skills or in what direction to go; you may learn the specific needs of the person listening to the tape. For example, he or she might need a song for a teen-oriented rock group, a duet or a female R& B singer.

Outside of bringing a good quality demo tape and any print materials that would be of interest (such as your bio, or the bio of the artist if you're also trying to land a record deal), there's not much else you can do to prepare for your meeting. Don't be late, of course, although you should not be discouraged if the person you're seeing keeps you waiting. It's to be expected, and it happens quite often, just as appointments are cancelled. Don't take any of this personally if it should happen to you. Remember, the people who can help you are busy, and in their minds, pressing matters take precedence over listening to new songs. They could just as easily request you send in or leave off a tape. But if they did grant you a personal appointment, then you just have to put up with whatever it is that annoys you.

There's no need to be nervous about the meeting. After all, the work (making the demo) is already done. All you have to do is be polite, hand over your demo to be played, get feedback (hopefully good), and leave (perhaps with an offer, or 'I like it. Let me live with it for a while and get back to you'). If you're an effervescent, energetic soul, pour on the charm and make a lasting (good) impression. Size up the listener. If there's good chemistry between you, you might have a friend and advisor, if not a 'buyer.'

Don't argue or try to defend your song if the feedback you get is negative. You're not going to change his mind whatever you say, and you don't want to close a door that might be open to you in the future. After your emotions subside, you might heed what the person said and consider revamping your song. Or you can disregard his criticism and go elsewhere. But no matter how angry, upset or frustrated you get, the professional thing to do is to keep your comments to yourself.

And remember that no one person's opinion is gospel. Every person has his own taste, and if yours just happens not to coincide with his, then move on to the next.

It is usually very difficult to get appointments with publishers, producers and A& R people. But it can be done and you can do it. You're going to have to be very persistent, though—much more so than the average 'salesperson.' Even professionals have to adopt this quality in their work.

You have to be persistent, and perhaps a little creative, to get your foot in the door. If you just cannot get a personal appointment, then you'll have to post your material. This is not to say that posting is bad; it can result in deals. It's just that a letter cannot replace personal contact.

When posting, be sure to enclose a self-addressed envelope. You'll have to go to the post office (if you don't have scales at home or in the office), because you will need to include return postage for the tape and a letter in your self-addressed envelope.

Your tape, covering letter, self-addressed envelope and any other materials you want to include, should be inserted neatly into your envelope. Be sure to write your return address on the envelope, also. And once again, if you are an artist or your demos have been recorded by a group of which you are a member, it would be appropriate to submit a photograph and bio(s).

Devising new strategies

Should your song not get placed anywhere, you should try to analyze why. Is the feedback you're getting pretty much the same? Are people making suggestions that they think might improve your song? If so, then perhaps you should rewrite it and cut another demo. You should also consider other options: you can record the song over again in a different arrangement or musical style. You can substitute a male singer for a female, or vice versa. If your song has been turned down by dozens of people, then the best thing to do is put it aside for a while and go on to another one. You should always be improving your technique and writing new material. As often happens, you'll probably like your latest songs best, and be excited about making demos of them.

CHAPTER NINE

KEEPING RECORDS

A successful songwriter is an organized individual. At least, songwriters who are organized are maximizing their chances for success. With the multitude of record producers, artists, A& R people, managers, agents, entertainment lawyers and other contacts in the music business, it becomes necessary to keep careful records of who you are submitting songs to,dates, and follow-up status.

The importance of maintaining careful records

It may take several submissions before your songs are accepted. Considering that obtaining appointments often requires persistent phoning to reach people in their offices, or that drawing attention to your mailed-in demo buried in a large stack of tapes may require several follow-up phone calls, it's necessary to keep diaries or logs of your business activities.

Keeping records of your activities is easy, but nonetheless requires commitment and discipline. Songwriters by nature want to orient their time and effort toward creative pursuits, not paperwork. But until you can get to see the people you want without too much difficulty you must be efficient in regard to making appointments and keeping track of your submissions.

Record-keeping may range from a simple diary of all activities in a notebook, to devising and maintaining 'systems' for efficient insertion of information. You may create your own and tailor them to your individual needs. Three are offered later in this chapter, for you to use or base your own on.

Meeting the right people

As discussed in Chapter Eight, 'Submitting Your Demos,' playing demos at a personal appointment is the best way to present material;

at least you know it is heard, and you can get professional feedback (albeit only one person's opinion) on the spot. Getting the appointments, however, may prove difficult.

In the quest to get your songs recorded, you will want to see the top producers, record company people and others. After all, they are in a position to record your songs with some of the best talent around, and if you think highly enough of your material (and you should if you will be going to all this trouble), then it only makes sense that you go after these people. (This is not to say that you should overlook others in a position to further your career).

Don't be intimidated by the success of those whom you seek out. At one time they were just starting out in the business too, and they will empathize (if they are down-to-earth) with your position. Furthermore, they *need* hits, and are always on the lookout for great material. They never know where it's going to come from, and *you* could be a fresh source. The trouble is, they are very busy, and have limited time set aside for appointments and auditioning new material.

Setting up appointments

Although you will not personally know the people you will want to see (and vice versa), the chances are that in most cases you can get in if you are persistent and approach the situation courteously and intelligently. If you call, you will invariably get one of the following responses: (1) so-and-so is not in or is in a meeting, and he doesn't take appointments anyway, so send in your material; (2) so-and-so is not in or is busy, so call back or leave your number and he/she will call you back; (3)yes, he is in, hold on please.

Reality being what it is, the last response is the one you are least likely to receive. If you should get through, give a presentation that is so irresistible that the person will *have* to give you a personal appointment. Give your name and say that you're a songwriter who has written one (or two or three) songs with tremendous hit potential for an artist with whom the person you're calling is associated. Say that you went to such great expense to make the demo that you just cannot leave it off, and that you must be present when it is played. Furthermore, as a prolific songwriter, it would mean a great deal to you to meet that person. You would be available anytime at his or her convenience, day or night (within reason), and would be extremely grateful for the opportunity to be heard. Said sincerely, this 'pitch' will be hard to resist. At this point you are in your salesperson's shoes, and have to be convincing, but never beg or sound desperate! If it works, good luck; if not and you're told to send your material in, well, then you'll just have to do that. But ask whoever you speak with to see to it personally that your demo gets played.

If the person you want to meet with is not in, you may leave your phone number. But if you don't get a return call within a reasonable period of time, call back. Call repeatedly if you have to. If this is a person you really must see, who could get your song right to the artist for whom you think it would be suitable, forget pride and personal feelings. Call and call until you get to speak to him or her. Just be courteous to the secretary or assistant with whom you talk. As a matter of fact, be friendly. If you could develop some kind of rapport with this person, he or she will see to it that you eventually get through. If you are rude, the person will get annoyed, and it will be very uncomfortable for you to call back again or a couple of times after, let alone several times. In addition, the secretaries and assistants of today will probably be powerful executives in the future, so it can't hurt to become friends with them.

If the person doesn't generally take appointments, then you can use the tactic described above—that you just cannot send your material in and that you would meet *anytime* at the convenience of the person with whom you want to meet. You'd be happy to keep on calling back until an appointment could be set up. Sometimes this will work, sometimes not. The chances are in your favour when you are convincing, polite, and perhaps have an overtone of urgency.

Logging your progress

As you can see, you may have to make a lot of phone calls, submissions and appointments. Keeping careful records is important. Examples of forms you could use to keep track of things are included here.

TELEPHONE RECORD—SAMPLE SHEET

DATE CALLED	NAME	COMPANY OR AFFILIATION	TELEPHONE NUMBER	SONGS	ARTIST	OUTCOME OF CALL

APPOINTMENTS RECORD—SAMPLE SHEET

DATE OF APPOINTMENT	NAME	COMPANY OR AFFILIATION	ADDRESS/ PHONE NO.	SONGS	ARTIST	OUTCOME OF MEETING AND PERSONAL COMMENT

SUBMISSIONS RECORD—SAMPLE SHEET

DATE POSTED	NAME	COMPANY OR AFFILIATION	ADDRESS/ PHONE NO.	SONGS SUBMITTED	ARTIST	RESPONSE

Another method of keeping records of material submitted by post is to have a separate sheet for each song, as follows*:

Song title _____

Date of Composition _____

Songwriter(s)

Name _____   Name_____

Address _____   Address _____

_____   _____

Phone _____   Phone _____

Publisher

Name _____   Name_____

Address _____   Address _____

_____   _____

Phone _____   Phone _____

Contact _____   Contact _____

Producer

Name _____   Name_____

Address _____   Address _____

_____   _____

Phone _____   Phone _____

Contact _____   Contact _____

Record Company

Name _____   Name_____

Address _____   Address _____

_____   _____

Phone _____   Phone _____

Contact _____   Contact _____

Forms like these should enable you to maintain an orderly check on your calls and submissions, and let you determine when it's time to call someone again or follow up on a submission. You can either make your own forms up, or photocopy these guidelines. The

*From Professional Music Manager by Henry Stephens, reproduced by permission of Music Soft, P.O. Box 2184, Jamaica, New York 11431.

records can be structured to meet your personal needs or style. The point is, do keep records. By looking at them, you'll know if you're working hard enough for your songs. Do it right, and it can only help your career.

CHAPTER TEN

A FINAL WORD (OR TWO...)

By now you should be familiar with multitrack recording, studios, MIDI, sequencers and other subjects covered in this book. As mentioned several times throughout the text, your real knowledge of techniques and technology will come from actual experience. No matter how much theory you instill in a medical student, without a body for 'hands on' experience, he'll never learn his subject fully, or derive the thrill of accomplishing what he's been trained for. The same may be said of songwriter-musician/recordists.

What I would like to address now is the question 'What does it take to be a professional songwriter?' Stated another way: 'What does it take to be a successful songwriter?' Talent—yes. Technical knowledge—it helps a great deal. The ability to sing—ditto. Assuming you have these qualities—at least the first!—let me discuss a non-musical but essential attribute—the 'right' attitude.'

Your attitude will determine how long you stick with the songwriting 'game,' how you make and cultivate contacts, how you cope with rejection, how you (enthusiastically or not) do your 'research' in finding markets to send your songs to, how others see your talent, and more. By attitude, I mean a composite of various qualities; perseverance, sensibility, ambition, energy, spirit, enthusiasm, vigour, resoluteness and enterprise. It's enough to ask that songwriters be talented, but to ask them also to be ideal beings ... well, that's certainly asking for a lot.

For the successful songwriter, however, the above qualities are requisite. This is because of the nature of the beast (the music business). In Chapter One, we saw that you're competing with established greats to get your songs on the charts. Artists aren't looking for album cuts. They want hits.

Therefore you must want to be a songwriter very badly. You have to view songwriting as a serious career if you wish to succeed. You're going to have to make phone calls, write letters, go to meetings, read the trades, study the charts, be an astute listener, learn wherever and whatever you can, make contacts, keep records of your submissions, spend money, endure criticism, face rejection, and suffer disappointment. Why go through all this?

Because you love music and you think you can write (or have written) some damn good songs—songs as good as or better than what's out there (remember, however, that subjectivity can be a dangerous thing). Because you don't want to sell insurance for a living. Because you want to become part of an exciting field. Because no other endeavour can give you the satisfaction that you get from creating sounds and words that can brighten people's days or lives.

So if you want to be a songwriter, a successful songwriter that is, you have to be willing to endure until you get that first cut. It's a survival of the fittest situation, because those who are not willing to persist despite all obstacles and rejections and psychological impairments will become songwriter drop-outs.

To endure means to believe in yourself, and if you believe in yourself then you will have the right attitude.

Add another characteristic to the list: aggressiveness. Yes, you must be assertive in getting your songs heard. To reach all the right people with your songs, you might have to cajole, plead and imploringly state your case. Songwriters have been known to go to elaborate measures to get certain individuals to hear their tunes.

Even after you get your first song recorded, your days of stroking music industry people's egos won't be over. The fate of your next tune will depend on the merits of that tune. But perhaps it will be easier to get through doors. A charted song is a great calling card. You might even have an exclusive songwriter's agreement with an important publisher, so you'll be able to send them all your songs and let the company do the leg-work to get the material placed.

If you think you have the ability to write consistently terrific, commercial songs, if music is a career you really want, if you're willing to endure some lean years in the hope that your songwriting talent will eventually bear fruit, then go on and do it! Remember, the precepts stated in this book, and *make great demos!* They're the passport to your future.

GLOSSARY

Acoustics. The qualities of a room or area, with its elements of design, construction and materials, that influence or shape the way that sound is heard.

Acoustical Musical Instrument. Any instrument that can be played without the use of electricity. Pianos, clarinets, trumpets, flutes, violins, cellos and drums—among others—are acoustical musical instruments.

Baffle. A partition, used in recording, that is hard (reflective) on one side and sound-absorbent ('dead') on the other. The hard side may have a wood surface: the absorbent side may be covered by fabric.

Basic Tracks. The first tracks recorded on multitrack tape. These tracks are the foundation of a recording and are those on which other performers subsequently overdub their parts. Basic tracks usually consist of a rhythm section—piano, bass, guitar, and drums.

Bounce. To transfer a track by mixing it with another in order to open up the track to record a part.

Dead. Non-reflective. Refers to an area of a studio that has padded surfaces to absorb reflections of sound.

Demo. An unfinished recording used to show the potential of a song or the tape embodying such a recording. A demo tape may contain one or more songs. Today, demos are usually presented in cassette format.

Electronic Musical Instruments. This term generally refers to instruments using computer technology, such as synthesizers and drum machines. It may be differentiated from electrical musical instruments, such as guitars, that use a current for amplification.

Expander. A sound-generating unit, or module, with no performer interface — essentially, a synthesizer (or sampler) without a keyboard. An expander produces sounds through the use of MIDI.

Lead Sheet. A handwritten musical notation of a song, with melody and chords; lyrics, title, author(s) of the song, and the copyright notice are also included.

Live. Reflective. Refers to an area of a studio that has hard, reflective surfaces, such as wood.

Magnetic Tape. A clear film base coated with a mixture of magnetic particles made up of gamma ferric oxide and other additives.

Master. The multitrack tape used to record, or the 2-track stereo tape that has been mixed down from the multitrack tape.

MIDI. Musical Instrument Digital Interface. A microprocessor communications network that allows electronic musical instruments of the same or different manufacturers to interconnect or receive performance data from one another, enabling a single individual playing a 'controller' to generate sounds from other instruments.

Mix. To blend the separately recorded sounds on a multitrack tape down to a 2-track stereo tape.

Mixing Console. A complex electronic device through which audio signals travel in tape recording and mixing, and that can be used to control, modify and route the signals. In recording, the signals are processed by the mixer but recorded by a separate multitrack tape recorder. In mixing, the tape recorder plays back the signals, and the mixing console is used to process them as they are recorded onto a 2-track stereo (mixdown) tape recorder. A mixing console is also known as a recording console, console, or board.

Monitor. A speaker. Recording studios usually have different size monitors to play back and hear how mixes sound on them. This shows how a mix would sound on any playback system such as a car or home stereo system, or portable cassette.

Multitrack Recording. The process or result of recording sounds (various instruments or voices, or both) onto separate storage spaces (tracks) of a tape.

Multitrack Tape Recorder. A tape recorder capable of recording more than one track; the number it can record depends on the type of machine. There are 2-track, 4-track, 8-track, 16-track, and 24-track tape recorders. Additional tracks may be obtained by 'locking up' two tape recorders, in synchronization.

Outboard Gear. Signal processors, such as compressor/limiters, noise gates, and reverb units, which are used to enhance recorded sound.

Overdub. To record a part over the basic tracks.

Recording Studio. A professional facility for recording music that consists of an area where performances are recorded (the studio) and an adjacent room where the engineer and producer control the flow of signal onto tape (the control room).

Reference Track. A track onto which a vocalist sings a song during the recording of the basic tracks in order to guide the other performers in recording their parts. The reference track, sometimes called a guide vocal, is subsequently erased and the lead vocal re-recorded.

Sequencer. A MIDI event recorder that can store, edit and play back performance data.

Session. A time-period during which musical material is recorded. Also called a recording session.

Slave. Any musical instrument or device playing data received from an external MIDI instrument or device, (the 'master').

Track. A portion of a multitrack tape onto which sound can be recorded.

APPENDIX

Demo checklist

Writing and arranging a song

1. Listen to the radio to stay current with what kinds of songs are 'making it.'
2. Develop a good idea into a well-crafted song.
3. Limit your song to three-and-a-half or four minutes.
4. Limit your introduction to four bars.
5. Do not have a long instrumental break or riff.
6. Have a contemporary arrangement, with a catchy 'sound' or groove.
7. Write mostly in the genre of music you're best at, and maximize your skills in that area.

Planning a demo—musical considerations

1. Make sure your song is complete and in optimum shape before demoing.
2. Get feedback from others, if you are unsure about a song's potential, before spending money to demo it.
3. Record only those songs with commercial potential.
4. Seek competent musicians if you need assistance in singing, playing, arranging and producing your song.

Planning a demo—business considerations

1. Negotiate fees and terms, and put these in writing if employing others.
2. Check a number of studios and compare their rates, payment schedules, availability, facilities and services.
3. Inquire if 'down time' is available in the studios you like.

4.   Ascertain all fees for talent, studio rental and materials, and devise a budget.

5.   Be sure you have enough money to pay all costs.

6.   Consider purchasing multitrack recording equipment instead of booking a professional studio and paying musicians.

Planning a demo—recording considerations

1.   Determine what instruments and vocal parts you'll be using.

2.   Figure out how many tracks you will need.

3.   Determine the order in which you'll be laying down the tracks.

4.   Consider the signal processing options available: compressing, limiting, noise gates, reverb.

5.   Ask an engineer questions about whatever you do not understand.

Protecting your song

Do any one of the following:

1.   Lodge a dated copy of your song with a bank or solicitor.

2.   Send a copy of your song to yourself by registered post.

3.   Have your song entered on the private registry at Stationers' Hall.

Preparing your demo for submission

1.   Use quality cassette tapes (30- and 60-minute tapes are best; shorter tapes are difficult to find on the consumer market, but are fine to use; 120-minute tapes are thin, and tend to stretch, rip, bleed, break, or jam).

2.   Put no more than four songs (unless otherwise instructed) on the tape.

3.   Put your best songs up front.

4.   Play the tape once through again to make sure all the sounds are bright and clear.

5.   Rewind the tape ready to play the first song.

6.   Pull out the 'record' tabs of the cassette.

7. Print clearly your name, telephone number, address, the names of the songs, and the copyright notice on the cassette label and on the paper label that goes into the cassette box.

8. Insert the cassette into a plastic container (soft plastic cases are better than hard boxes because they won't crush or break through envelopes).

Finding markets

1. 'Cast' your song—try to decide which artists would be most suitable for recording it.

2. Look for new markets—read the music press, read album covers, listen to the radio, study the record charts.

3. Consider all possibilities, including music publishers, producers, labels, managers, agents and lawyers.

4. Make personal appointments to play your demo when possible.

Sending your package

1. Send three items: your demo, a typed (or neatly written) covering letter and a self-addressed envelope.

2. Be sure your name, address and telephone number are included in the covering letter.

3. Send your package to the attention of a specific person.

4. Include a photograph and bio if you are pitching yourself as an artist as well.

5. Include the correct postage for the SAE.

Keeping records

1. Compile a list of every artist, producer, publisher and label to whom you want to submit.

2. Develop a system to notate every submission.

3. Follow up if you haven't had a response in four weeks.

4. Keep a log of every phone call you make, noting secretaries' names and when you should call back..

5. Keep records of each party's feedback or response.

6. Understand that the submission process is arduous and discouraging, and develop a positive mental attitude.

INDEX

If you have enjoyed this book you will also be interested in the following Omnibus Press titles.

THE CRAFT OF GREAT LYRIC WRITING
Sheila Davis
ISBN: 0.7119.1718.3
Order No: OP 45152

MAKING MONEY MAKING MUSIC
James W. Dearing
ISBN: 0.7119.1721.3
Order No: OP 45186

THE SONGWRITER'S AND MUSICIAN'S GUIDE TO MAKING GREAT DEMOS
Harvey Rachlin
ISBN: 0.7119.1715.9
Order No: OP 45129

MAKING IT IN THE NEW MUSIC BUSINESS
James Riordan
ISBN: 0.7119.1717.5
Order No: OP 45145

WRITING TOGETHER: THE SONGWRITER'S GUIDE TO COLLABORATION
Walter Carter
ISBN: 0.7119.1713.2
Order No: OP 45103

SUCCESSFUL LYRIC WRITING: STEP-BY-STEP COURSE & WORKSHOP
Sheila Davis
ISBN: 0.7119.1720.5
Order No: OP 45178

PROFIT FROM YOUR MUSIC
James Gibson
ISBN: 0.7119.1716.7
Order No: OP 45137

GETTING NOTICED: THE MUSICIAN'S GUIDE TO PUBLICITY AND SELF PROMOTION
James Gibson
ISBN: 0.7119.1719.1
Order No: OP 45160

HOW TO PITCH & PROMOTE YOUR SONGS
Fred Koller
ISBN: 0.7119.1714.0
Order No: OP 45111

THE CRAFT & BUSINESS OF SONGWRITING
John Braheny
ISBN: 0.7119.1820.1
Order No: OP 45418

BREAKS FOR YOUNG BANDS
Ed Berman
ISBN: 0.7119.0978.4
Order No: OP 43926

HOW TO MAKE AND SELL YOUR OWN RECORD
Diane Sward Rapaport
ISBN: 0.7119.0759.5
Order No: AM 39785

HOW TO SUCCEED IN THE MUSIC BUSINESS
Allan Dann & John Underwood
ISBN: 0.86001.454.1
Order No: AM 19977

PLATINUM RAINBOW: HOW TO MAKE IT BIG IN THE MUSIC BUSINESS
Bob Monaco & James Riordan
ISBN: 0.7119.1040.5
Order No: 44130

Omnibus Press
No. 1 for Rock & Pop Books